Copyright © 2002, 2003 Roger Sapp. All rights reserv~ ~~~~~~~~~~~~~~ ~~
protected under the copyright laws of the United States of America. This study
guide may not be copied or reprinted without written permission of the author.
Reproduction or duplication of this text without written permission of the author
for any reason or any use is both illegal and unethical. Permission may be granted
on request for unusual circumstances.

Order this **Self-Study Course**
(formerly called Study Guide)
(**ISBN: 0-9702341-4-7**)

and the companion volume
Performing Miracles and Healing

from:
All Nations Publications
P.O. Box 92847
Southlake, Texas 76092
United States of America
1-817-514-0653

or
from our secure website:
www.allnationsmin.org

Printed in the United States by Morris Publishing
3212 East Highway 30
Kearney, NE 68847
1-800-650-7888

Table of Contents

Introduction

1. How does the author, Dr. Roger Sapp, describe his theology of healing before 1992? Pg. 1

_____

_____

2. The author describes his experience of healing before 1992? Pg. 1

_____

_____

3. What caused The author to have a personal breakthrough on the matter of healing? Pg. 1

_____

_____

4. What did he discover in his subsequent study of Scripture on the matter of healing? Pg. 1-2

_____

_____

_____

5. What was most apparent to him about his beliefs as he discovered that he could not reconcile what he believed with Scripture? Pg. 2

_____

_____

_____

6. What place did Jesus Christ have in the author's previous theology of healing? Pg. 2

_____

_____

_____

7. What had the author's previous theology of healing relied upon? Pg. 2.

_____

_____

_____

8. The author says that he knew more about the common explanations of the value of suffering than he knew about what? Pg. 3.

9. How did having his theology of healing transformed affect his experience of healing within the first few months? Pg. 3.

_____

_____

_____

10. What happened within a couple of years? Pg. 3

_____

_____

11. How does the author demonstrate Christ's willingness to heal? Pg. 3-4

_____

_____

_____

_____

12. The author says that the focus on his ministry is not healing the sick but is rather what? Pg. 4

_____

_____

13. What does the author say is his hope for the readers of his book? Pg. 4-5

_____

_____

_____

14. In the context of the end of the age, what must the Church do? Pg. 5.

_____

_____

15. Why must Christ-like power in healing and miracles punctuate the Gospel at the end of the age? Pg. 5

_____

_____

Chapter One
Christ Reveals the Father

1. The author declares that there is a biblical truth that is a foundation to consistently healing the sick and injured. What does he predict about any ministry that misses this truth? Pg. 4

_____

_____

2. What causes this foundational truth to be taken for granted and underestimated in significance? Pg. 4

_____

_____

3. What is the main reason why healing and miracle ministry is not found consistently in the lives of many Church leaders? Pg. 4

_____

_____

4. What book of the Bible expresses this important truth more often than any other? Pg. 4

_____

_____

5. To know Christ is to know what? Pg. 5

_____

_____

6. What will studying the life of Christ reveal? Pg. 5

_____

_____

7. If Christians fail to believe that Christ expresses the will of the Father perfectly what will happen in the area of healing for them? Pg. 5

_____

_____

8. The author says that the Bible declares God's will and purpose. However, much of that will and purpose was unclear and unrevealed until what? Pg. 5-6

_____

_____

9. What has happen to mysteries that once were hidden? Pg. 6

_____

_____

10. Christ tells Philip in John Chapter 14 that when He (Christ) is seen, who is seen? Pg. 6

_____

_____

11. Every verbal expression of Christ and action of Christ reveals what? Pg. 6

_____

_____

12. What must we believe in to do the works of Christ in healing? Pg. 6

_____

_____

_____

_____

13. Christ does not speak on His own initiative. What does this imply? Pg. 6

_____

_____

14. The Father in Christ does the works. What does this mean? Pg. 7

_____

_____

_____

_____

15. According to John Chapter 14, Faith in Christ must include what? Pg. 7

_____

_____

16. If believers fail to believe that Christ reveals the will and nature of the Father what will they find difficult? Pg. 7

_____

_____

17. What can be discerned from observing the works of Christ? Pg. 8

_____

_____

18. Christ promises that we can do His works. What earlier statement is this promise conditioned upon? Pg. 8

_____

_____

19. If believers express the will of the Father as Christ did, what will they do? Pg. 8

_____

_____

20. What are the conditions of Christ's promise of "greater works" in this passage? Pg. 8

_____

_____

_____

_____

21. What must believers believe about the will of the Father? Pg. 8

_____

_____

22. Now that Christ has gone to the Father, what is happening? Pg. 8

_____

_____

23. What does the author say is foundational to accomplishing similar or greater things in ministry as Christ? Pg. 8

_____

_____

_____

_____

24. What causes the failure of much theology and practice to duplicate Christ's supernatural ministry? Pg. 8

_____

_____

25. In John Chapter 6, Christ's disciples ask Him an important question. What is the question? Pg. 9

_____

_____

26. How does the author rephrase it? Pg. 9

_____

_____

_____

_____

27. What is Christ's answer to this important question? Pg. 9

_____

_____

28. The author says that the last part of Christ's answer is more important than the first part. How does the author restate what Christ has said? Pg. 9

_____

_____

29. The author says that a general unspecified faith in Christ is not significant in this passage. What kind of faith is significant? Pg. 9

_____

_____

30. In a short passage in John Chapter 8, three important elements are revealed. Because Christ did not initiate the things that He did, then believers can learn one of these things about the will of the Father from doing what? Pg. 9-10

_____

_____

_____

_____

31. Christ only spoke the things that the Father taught Him. Therefore, believers can learn about the Father's will by doing what? Pg. 10

_____

_____

32. What does most modern theology do with what Christ said about healing or what He said before and after He healed people? Pg. 10

_____

_____

33. Since Christ only did those things that pleased the Father, what can be said about the various healings and miracles in His ministry? Pg. 10

_____

_____

34. What else does the author says that must be recognized in the healing and miracle matters of Christ's ministry? Pg. 10

_____

_____

35. Teaching on healing that advocates ideas, attitudes, and actions that do not find their basis in Christ Himself will fail to do what? Pg. 10

_____

_____

36. What does the author says is highly appropriate and will be discussed throughout his book? Pg. 10

_____

_____

_____

_____

37. The author presents a passage in John Chapter 5 that he says that some have misunderstood. What is it that they have misunderstood? Pg. 11

_____

_____

_____

_____

38. The author says that Christ had previously and already done what? Pg. 11

_____

_____

_____

_____

39. As Christ acted upon what He had previously seen the Father doing, what happened? Pg. 11

_____

_____

40. Most people in Christ's ministry were healed in what normal way? Pg. 11-12

_____

_____

41. When one wishes to know the will of the Father concerning a matter what should your first observation be? Pg. 12

_____

_____

42. What does the author say is amazing? Pg. 12

_____

_____

43. According to John 5:30 and John 6:38, whose will did Christ seek and do? Pg. 12

_____

_____

44. According to John 8:26-27, John 8:40, and John 17:14, where did Christ hear the things that He spoke? Pg. 12-13

_____

_____

45. What did Christ insist upon in John 7:29, John 10:15a and John 8:55? Pg.13

_____

_____

46. Whose works was Christ accomplishing according to John 5:36b-37a and John 4:34? Pg. 13

_____

_____

47. Why does author says that it is significant that the Gospel of John was the last book of the Bible written to the Church? Pg. 14

_____

_____

48. If believers fail to grasp how significant this truth of Christ being a pure reflection of the Father what will happen? Pg. 14

_____

_____

49. What is the key to working the works of God? Pg. 14

_____

_____

50. What do Colossians 1:15 and Colossians 2:9 reveal? Pg. 14

_____

_____

51. The first chapter of the book of Hebrews offers some comparisons from the Old Testament with Christ. What are they? Pg. 14-15

_____

_____

_____

_____

52. The writer of Hebrews tells us that Christ is the radiance of the Father's glory. What other translations of "radiance" would be appropriate here? Pg. 15

_____

_____

53. The writer of Hebrews also tells us that Christ is the "exact representation of the Father's nature". What other translations would be appropriate in this verse? Pg. 15-16

_____

_____

_____

_____

54. The author suggests that no theology of healing should ever be formed without doing what? Pg. 16

_____

_____

_____

_____

55. The foundation of a proper theology of healing must be built on what? Pg .16

_____

_____

56. What is a "Christocentric theology"? Pg. 16

_____

_____

57. Any healing theology that is not "Christocentric" will not do what? Pg. 16

_____

_____

58. What happens to people who embrace "murky" theology that do not clearly express the will of the Father in these matters? Pg. 16

_____

_____

_____

_____

59. Try to form a theology of healing without Christ is similar to forming a theology of salvation without what? Pg .17

_____

_____

60. Some leaders retain the reasoning and attitudes that accompany false doctrines that they have rejected concerning healing that affects their theology specifically in healing and miracles. The author says they have what? Pg. 17

_____

_____

61. What kind of atmosphere does this "murky" theology about healing create? Pg. 18

_____

_____

62. How is this atmosphere reinforced? What does it suggest? Pg. 18

_____

_____

_____

_____

63. What does the author say is entirely appropriate to examine in the next chapters? Pg. 18

_____

_____

Chapter Two
Christ's Ministry to the Masses in Matthew and Mark

1. Why should the will of the Father be clear to believers? Pg. 20

_____

_____

2. Why is the will of the Father not clear nevertheless to many people? Pg. 20

_____

_____

_____

_____

3. What is one of the objectives of the book? Pg. 20

_____

_____

_____

_____

4. In this analysis, what is important to discover? Pg. 20

_____

_____

_____

_____

5. The actual study begins with "general descriptions" of Christ's ministry. What does the author mean by "general descriptions"? Pg. 20

_____

_____

_____

_____

6. The general description found in Matthew 4:23-24 reveals the activity of healing in the ministry of Christ in the context of what three other activities? Pg. 21

_____

_____

7. How is "proclaiming" translated in some versions? Pg. 21

_____

_____

8. What is significant about Christ healing "every kind of disease and every kind of sickness"? Pg. 21

_____

_____

9. What is absent from this account that is significant as well? Pg. 21-22

_____

_____

10. What does Christ not do that is significant? Pg. 22

_____

_____

11. The general description found in Matthew 4:23-24 reveals five different kinds of problems that Christ healed. What were they? Pg. 22

_____

_____

12. The author notes what special category as being interesting? Pg. 22

_____

_____

13. How many of what particular group does the passage strongly imply were healed? Pg. 22

_____

_____

14. Fill in the blank: What is absent in this general account is any _____ in the ministry of Christ toward healing the sick. Pg. 22

_____

15. Fill in the blank: There is no _____ of the will of God in each situation for each person. Pg. 22

_____

16. Fill in the blank: There seems to be no _____ of people into categories of those who should be healed and those who should not be healed. Pg. 22

_____

17. The second general description of the ministry of Christ found in Matthew's Gospel contains an important quotation from what Old Testament book? Pg. 22

_____

_____

18. Casting out demons through a word implies what? Pg. 23

_____

_____

19. This method of casting out demons appears where else in Scripture? Pg. 23

_____

_____

20. How many were healed in this situation? Pg. 23

_____

_____

21. Many were brought to Christ and all were healed. This means that there is no evidence of what? Pg. 23

_____

_____

_____

_____

22. What does Christ healing "all" among the "many" in this situation mean? Pg. 23

_____

_____

23. Not a single person demonstrated what? Pg. 23

_____

_____

24. What did Matthew reveal about this example of healing ministry? Pg. 23

_____

_____

_____

_____

25. Why is this prophecy highly significant? Pg. 23

_____

_____

_____

_____

26. This passage substantiates that when Christ died for our sins at the cross, what else did He do for us? Pg. 23-24

_____

_____

27. What is also significant in producing consistent results in healing ministry? Pg. 24

_____

_____

28. What is notably absent from this account? Pg. 24

_____

_____

29. The author notes that three elements are often found together. What are they? Pg. 24

_____

_____

30. Healing and casting out demons are possible to accomplish without do what particular activities? Pg. 24

_____

_____

31. What is absent from this account? Pg. 24

_____

_____

32. From anyone's way of accounting, what was the Father's will in this situation? Pg. 24

_____

_____

33. In the third general account found in Matthew 9:35, healing occurred in what context? Pg. 24

_____

_____

34. What does Christ healing every kind of disease and every kind of sickness logically imply? Pg. 24

_____

_____

35. What was not displayed in Christ's ministry that seems to be imposed by some modern theologies upon those who seek to heal the sick today? Pg. 24-25

_____

_____

36. What would happen to an identical ministry to Christ's today in many churches? Pg. 25

_____

_____

37. How would some ministers today consider a ministry similar to Christ's ministry? Pg. 25

_____

_____

38. Why are things changing dramatically? Pg. 25

39. Fill in the blank: The supernatural ministry of Christ is being _____ and experienced in many places as it should. Pg. 25

_____

40. Where and when did the events found in the fourth general description in Matthew's Gospel take place? Pg. 25

_____

_____

41. The people who were healed in this general description were included in what other miracle? Pg. 25

_____

_____

42. How did the author at the assumption that there were at least 6,000 people present during this healing event? Pg. 25

_____

_____

_____

_____

43. How did the author arrive at "more than 600 people with healing needs in this one situation"? Pg. 25-26

_____

_____

_____

_____

44. What does the author believe about this estimation? Pg. 26

_____

_____

45. The passage does not focus so much on sickness but upon what? Pg. 26

_____

_____

46. What four conditions does it focus upon? Pg. 26

_____

_____

47. The author suggests that the New American Standard Bible should have translated the word here as "crippled" as what other English words? Pg. 26

_____

_____

48. What phrase allows for all other kinds of sickness and disease in this passage? Pg. 26

_____

_____

49. On average, how many of each of the five kinds of conditions can be estimated by using the previous estimates? Pg. 26

_____

_____

50. How long had the 4,000 plus people been with Christ? Pg. 27

_____

_____

51. This "three days" indicates what? Pg. 27

_____

_____

52. What does the passage not reveal? Pg. 27

_____

_____

53. If it was the Father's will for some to remain sick, injured or disabled, then what would have Christ have done? Pg. 27

_____

_____

54. Fill in the blank: This passage and many others will show that the Father's will for the sick, injured, and disabled is _____. Pg. 27

_____

55. The fifth general description of Christ's ministry to the masses found in Mark, Chapter 1, has more emphasis on what than Matthew's Gospel? Pg. 27

_____

_____

56. What does the fact that many who were ill and demonized were brought to Christ imply? Pg. 28

_____

_____

57. What does the passage say and not say concerning how many were healed? Pg. 28

_____

_____

58. What does the author say that there is not a hint of? Pg. 28

_____

_____

59. What does popular modern theology suggest is the Father's will? Pg. 28

_____

_____

60. What does unbelieving theology want to find in Mark's general description? Pg. 28

_____

_____

61. What does the passage actually say? Pg. 28

_____

_____

62. What does the author say is unlikely? Pg. 28

_____

_____

63. If Mark was trying to indicate that some were not healed, then logically the opposite of many being healed is what? Pg. 28

_____

_____

64. If allowance is made for a few not being healed, what does this not indicate? Pg. 28

_____

_____

65. Fill in the blanks: The Father's will is not fulfilled in _____ _____ _____ for various reasons. Pg. 28

_____

66. The author gives a number of examples of the Father's will not being fulfilled. What are they? Pg. 28

_____

_____

_____

_____

67. Someone not being healed on any particular occasion does not reveal what? Pg. 28

_____

_____

68. In this passage, the demons wanted to speak but Christ was doing what? Pg. 29

_____

_____

69. What two ministries were common elements in the ministry of Christ and His followers? Pg. 29

_____

_____

70. How were sickness, injury and demonic activity treated by Christ? Pg. 29

_____

_____

71. What is not found in the New Testament according to the author? Pg. 29

_____

_____

72. If nothing Christ says (or does) would encourage believers to another approach, then what should believers seek to do? Pg. 29

_____

_____

73. Where do other approaches come from? Pg. 29

_____

_____

74. So many people were being healed in the sixth general description of Christ's healing ministry, what was it necessary for Christ to do? Pg. 30

_____

_____

75. This passage again uses the term "many" which does not reveal what? Pg. 30

_____

_____

76. The passage does not imply what? Pg. 30

_____

_____

77. What is extremely doubtful when this passage is compared to other healing passages? Pg. 30

_____

_____

78. Fill in the blanks: The _____ on of _____ was a common way that Christ healed the sick. Pg. 30

_____

79. This passage (Mark 3:9-11) reveals that people were healed in another common way. Pg. 30

_____

_____

80. What does the author say might have been the reason that Christ did not allow the demons to speak at other times? Pg. 30

_____

_____

81. True or False? Mark's Gospel does record a general description of Christ's ministry to the masses where there were evidently people who were sick that were not healed. Pg. 30-31

_____

82. The seventh general description (Mark 6:2b-6a) of Christ's ministry to the masses takes place in what town? Pg. 31

_____

_____

83. In this circumstance, Christ announced what about Himself? Pg. 31

_____

_____

84. People in Christ's own hometown did not understand Him or His mission. How did they react to Him? Pg. 31

_____

_____

85. Why didn't these people see that Christ was revealing the will and power of the Father? Pg. 31

_____

_____

86. What does the great blessing of healing ministry often come with? Pg. 31

_____

_____

87. What is a small price to pay for the capacity to help many suffering people? Pg. 31

_____

_____

88. True or False? Christ was just as capable of helping people in His own hometown as elsewhere. Pg. 31

_____

89. What is there no mention of in this passage? Pg. 31-32

_____

_____

90. What does the context of the passage (Mark 6:2b-6a) reveal? Pg. 32

_____

_____

91. What does the statement in this passage also reveal? Pg. 32

_____

_____

92. What was different in this circumstance that created the seemingly powerlessness of Christ to help these people? Pg. 32

_____

_____

93. How did those who believed that Christ could help them react in other places? Pg. 32

_____

_____

94. Conversely, what was the reaction of the people to Christ is His hometown basically? Pg. 32

_____

_____

95. True or False? Because of their lack of faith, Christ was only able to help a few sick people and was unable to do any miracles. Pg. 32

_____

96. What is this event consistent with that will be observed in subsequent chapters? Pg. 32

_____

_____

Chapter Three
Christ's Ministry to the Masses in Luke, John and Acts

1. Which Gospel contains more general descriptions of Christ's ministry to the masses than any other? Pg. 33

_____

2. The eight general account of Christ ministry is Luke 4:40. Who does the "all" in this verse describe? Pg. 33

_____

_____

3. What methodology was Christ using in this passage to heal the sick? Pg. 33

_____

_____

4. The statement about Christ healing these people strongly implies what? Pg. 33

_____

_____

5. As in previous accounts, what is there no revelation of in this passage? Pg. 34

_____

_____

_____

_____

6. What happened when they encountered Christ? Pg. 34

_____

_____

7. Fill in the blanks: Christ never sends someone away with a _____ _____ _____ of how sickness is doing them some sort of good. Pg. 34

_____

8. True or False? The proclamation of the Gospel does not always accompany healing in Christ's ministry. Pg. 34

_____

9. True or False? Christ does not always heal the sick whenever and wherever they respond to Him in faith. Pg. 34

_____

10. The ninth general description is found in Luke 5:15-16. How is this passage similar to previous passages that we have studied? Pg. 34-35

_____

_____

11. Why will any dynamic healing ministry be able to draw a crowd when people really believe that something genuine is happening? Pg. 34

_____

_____

12. Fill in the blank: Healing ministry always has an _____ capacity that many other ministries lack. Pg. 34

_____

13. What was an important ingredient in the ongoing ministry of Christ to help people? Pg. 35

_____

_____

14. What is absent and not mentioned in this passage? Pg. 35

_____

_____

15. The tenth general account of Christ healing the masses is found in Luke's Gospel, Chapter 8. This passage also reveals that Christ did what activity shortly before the events took place? Pg. 35

_____

_____

16. How does this passage draw a distinction between the multitude of people coming to Jesus? Pg. 36

_____

_____

_____

17. What was the motive of both groups of people? Pg. 36

_____

_____

18. How can we tell if coming to hear Christ and to be healed are proper motives to come to Christ? Pg. 36

_____

_____

19. What do the writers of the Gospels repeatedly report? Pg. 36

20. What does Luke report that has been previously reported by Matthew and Mark? Pg. 36

_____

_____

21. What three ongoing, normal, and expected expressions of the ministry of Christ does the author list? Pg. 36

_____

_____

22. How does Luke describe Christ's dealing with demons in this passage (Luke 6:17-19)? Pg. 36

_____

_____

23. What does this description reveal about demons and their activity? Pg. 36

_____

_____

24. Where else is this truth revealed? Pg. 36

_____

_____

25. What makes the eleventh general description of Christ's ministry found in Luke 7:18-23 interesting? Pg. 36-37

_____

_____

26. What significant question did the disciples of John the Baptist ask Christ? Pg. 37

_____

_____

27. Christ's response to the question contains significant information on what? Pg. 37

_____

_____

_____

28. What does the context of this question reveal about the disciples of John the Baptist? Pg. 37

_____

_____

_____

_____

29. What does the phrase "the expected one" mean? Pg. 37

_____

_____

30. What happen to John's disciples after they asked the question? Pg. 37-38

_____

_____

31. At that time Christ cured many of four kinds of conditions. What conditions are mentioned? Pg. 38

_____

_____

32. What condition does this passage focus upon? Pg. 38

_____

_____

33. What does the phrase "granted sight" imply? Pg. 38

_____

_____

34. Why didn't Christ have total control? Pg. 38

_____

_____

35. This element of partial control is found in many passages and is what? Pg. 38

_____

_____

36. Why does the idea of partial control of healing create objections? Pg. 38

_____

_____

37. What does Christ tell John's disciples is the answer to their question? Pg. 38

_____

_____

38. Christ identifies some additional miraculous works that brings the total to eight. What eight conditions that He healed does Christ identify to John's disciples? Pg. 38-39

_____

39. The author asks a rhetorical question about Christ putting such a strong emphasis on the healing aspects of His ministry. What is the question? Pg. 39

_____

_____

_____

_____

40. What does the author speculate is the cause of many lost persons failing to recognize Christ in His Church? Pg. 39

_____

_____

41. Why do believers often fail at this? Pg. 39

_____

_____

42. Why do believers fail to act in faith? Pg. 39

_____

_____

43. What standard of comparison will show that some cautions that appear wise are not really wise? Pg. 39

_____

_____

44. What will the company of believers in the future be willing to risk? Pg. 39

_____

_____

45. What kind of insight will the passage in Luke 9:10b-11 give us into Christ's ministry? Pg. 39

_____

_____

46. What city did Christ privately withdraw to? Pg. 39-40

_____

_____

47. What happen when Christ tried to privately withdraw? Pg. 40

_____

_____

48. True or False? Christ refused to minister to these people because He had planned to withdraw. Pg. 40

49. What does this passage show about Christ's prior knowledge or revelation about every aspect of His ministry. Pg. 40

50. What did Christ already know about what the Father wanted for the sick and injured that did not require additional revelation? Pg. 40

51. What is repeatedly revealed in previous passages and this one? Pg. 40

52. In what context is healing revealed again? Pg. 40

53. True or False? Healing is sometimes found in passages without a reference to the Gospel. Pg. 41

54. True or False? Healing is frequently discovered in passages where the Gospel is being preached. Pg. 41

55. What does the statement "curing those who had need of healing" not allow? Pg. 41

56. Fill in the blank: Again, there is no_____ of people into categories of those who should be healed and those who should not be healed. Pg. 41.

57. What does Christ reveal about the will of the Father? Pg. 40

58. The thirteenth general description of Christ's healing ministry is easily overlooked. Luke describes the healing and miracles in Christ's ministry as being what? Pg. 41

59. The fourteenth description is a few verses later, in Luke 13:32. Christ describes His ministry to someone to pass the description to what important political figure? Pg. 41

_____

_____

60. Christ describes His ministry in what three parts? Pg. 41

_____

_____

61. What does Christ reveal that He does on the first two days "today and tomorrow"? Pg. 41

_____

_____

62. What does the third day relate to? Pg. 41

_____

_____

63. What idea that will be discussed later does the author says is important? Pg. 41

_____

_____

64. The other general descriptions of Christ's ministry written by Luke in the Book of Acts are placed at the end of the chapter. These passages could have followed Luke's Gospel but are placed after some passages in John's Gospel. Why? Pg. 41-42

_____

_____

65. Why does the author say that the few general descriptions of the mass ministry of Christ in the Gospel of John are less helpful overall? Pg. 42

_____

_____

66. The fifteenth general description of Christ's ministry is found in John 6:2. What does the author say is another place where what important element appears? Pg. 42

_____

_____

67. Why was Christ able to attract a multitude? Pg. 42

_____

_____

68. As the end of the age nears, what is there every reason to believe? Pg. 42

_____

_____

_____

_____

69. In what other way could the Greek word translated "performing" be translated? Pg. 43

_____

_____

70. What is completely opposite from the idea that healing ministry is unpredictable, unreliable and mysterious? Pg. 43

_____

_____

71. What does the author say is a common misconception about healing ministry? Pg. 43

_____

_____

72. What is the hope of the author for every reader of this book? Pg. 43

_____

_____

73. What is the foundation of being able to consistently perform healing? Pg. 43

_____

_____

74. What idea is prominent in the sixteenth general description of Christ's ministry found in John 7:31. Pg. 43

_____

_____

75. In this passage, why did many of the multitude believe in Him? Pg. 43

_____

_____

76. Without the capacity to perform miracles and healing what will the Church be unequipped to do? Pg. 44

_____

_____

77. True or False? Technique and polish are the answer to reaching the harvest. Pg. 44

_____

78. What was beyond the conception of the people in John 7:31? Pg. 44

_____

79. The sixteenth general description of Christ's healing ministry to the masses, found in John 12:37, sadly reveals what? Pg. 44

80. Fill in the blank: In this passage, John reveals that Christ had performed _____ signs. Pg. 44

_____

81. Miracle and healing ministry will always find opposition among what group? Pg. 45

_____

82. What will those who fail to become equipped in healing be tempted to do? Pg. 45

_____

83. The eighteenth general description of Christ's healing ministry to the masses is found in John 20:30-31. What should happen to anyone carefully, honestly, and logically considering these passages? Pg. 45

_____

84. True or False? The Bible records all the events of healing and miracles in the life of Christ. Pg. 45

_____

85. Why did the authors of the New Testament select certain events of healing and miracles? Pg. 45

_____

86. Many miracles and healings of Christ were not recorded by John's Gospel. What else does this imply and why? Pg. 46

_____

87. What was John's purpose in recording the miracles and healing of Jesus Christ? Pg. 46

_____

88. What have some critics of healing ministry suggested? Pg. 46

_____

89. If this were true, who would be in the category of the carnal? Pg. 46

_____

_____

90. Why would the apostle John not agree with these critics? Pg. 46

_____

_____

91. How old was John and how long had he reflected upon the ministry of Christ when the Gospel of John was written? Pg. 46

_____

92. The final group of passages that describe Christ's ministry to the masses are found in the Book of Acts. In the nineteenth general description, Peter is speaking in Acts 2:22 and reveals some important information about Christ. What do some believers seem to forget that this passage reveals? Pg. 47

_____

_____

93. Christ can only be the example is He is what? Pg. 47

_____

_____

94. What must seen and not be denied about Christ's nature? Pg. 47

_____

_____

_____

95. What is this foundational biblical truth called? Pg. 47

_____

_____

96. What must one recognize in order to do the greater works that Christ promises? Pg. 47

_____

_____

97. How did God (the Father) attest to the ministry of Christ and also to His disciples? Pg. 47

_____

_____

98. What should believers expect today? Pg. 47

_____

_____

99. How is the divine balance revealed in healing and miracle ministry? Pg. 48

_____

_____

100. What should healing and miracles produce in eyewitnesses? Pg. 48

_____

_____

101. Do eyewitnesses always become believers in Christ? Pg. 48

_____

_____

102. What have some Christians today been taught? Pg. 48

_____

_____

103. What will happen when Christ's church demonstrates His power at the end of the age? Pg. 48

_____

_____

104. The twentieth general description is found in Acts Chapter 10. Why is this the most general description that has been expressed? Pg. 48

_____

_____

_____

105. True or False? Understanding that Christ ministered miraculously as a human being is not essential in performing miracles and healing. Pg. 49

_____

106. Fill in the blanks: The Holy Spirit uses _____ _____ with all their flaws, failures and forgiven sins. Pg. 49

_____

107. What is not the only issue? Pg. 49

_____

_____

108. What are too many already anointed believers doing? Pg. 49

_____

_____

109. What is the consequence of passively waiting? Pg. 49

_____

_____

110. What is obviously connected throughout the New Testament with the Holy Spirit? Pg. 49

_____

_____

111. What two activities are connected with power in Acts 10:38? Pg. 49

_____

_____

112. If a person desires an example of what the Father considers good, what should they do? Pg. 50

_____

_____

113. What cannot be considered "doing good"? Pg. 50

_____

_____

114. What does the apostle Peter reveal just like the Gospel writers? Pg. 50

_____

_____

115. What does the term "healing" in this general description describe? Pg. 50

_____

_____

_____

116. What does the Greek word that is translated "oppressed" in this passage mean? Pg. 50

_____

_____

_____

117. What was Christ's healing overcoming? Pg. 50

_____

_____

118. What does the author say is simple and wonderfully profound? Pg. 50

_____

_____

_____

119. True or False? Christ was not using His own divine power but God the Father and the Holy Spirit were at work in Him. Pg. 50

_____

120. Fill in the blanks: Christ in the Scriptures is a _____ _____ by the Holy Spirit acting out the will of God the Father on earth. Pg. 50-51

_____

121. How many total general descriptions of Christ's ministry to the masses does the author list? Pg. 51

_____

_____

122. How many general descriptions mention preaching the Gospel? Pg. 51

_____

123. How many general descriptions mention something pertaining to demons, demoniacs or the devil? Pg. 51

_____

124. How many of the general descriptions specifically mention someone not being healed? Why weren't they healed? Pg. 51

_____

_____

125. Fill in the blanks: There is _____ _____ in any of these accounts that the will of the Father might be different for different people in the matter of healing. Pg. 51

_____

126. Fill in the blank: Christ _____ hesitates to heal someone in the passages that have been examined. Pg. 51

_____

127. Fill in the blanks: Christ_____ _____ what the will of the Father will be for the thousands of people He healed. Pg. 51

_____

128. Fill in the blanks: In some of the general events, the passages reveal that Christ _____ _____ that came to Him in a multitude. Pg. 51

_____

129. What is the impressive idea the author says is presented in a number of passages? Pg. 51

_____

_____

Chapter Four
The Twelve Apostles' Healing Ministry

1. According to the author, why is much theology concerning healing passive and impotent? Pg. 53

_____

_____

2. Fill in the blank: The Father's will is perfectly revealed through Christ's _____ to His disciples as well as it has been through His teaching, actions, works and attitudes. Pg. 54

_____

3. True or False? Real disciples must be the kind of believers that have real faith and work the works of God. Pg. 54

_____

4. What are modern believers often not taught to observe (obey)? Pg. 54

_____

_____

5. What were the Twelve disciples commissioned to do in Matthew 10:1, 5-8? Pg. 55

_____

_____

_____

_____

6. True or False? Every command to the Twelve apostles applies to every disciple in every generation because of the Great Commission. Pg. 55

_____

7. What is the only alternative to doing and to preaching what Christ commanded the Twelve to do? Pg. 56

_____

_____

8. What has the deceptive appearance of orthodoxy? Pg. 56

_____

_____

9. What have many respected leaders inherited? Pg. 56

_____

_____

10. What will those discipled by these respected ministers assume? Pg. 56

_____

_____

11. Fill in the blanks: Christ-like leaders can be good examples in some areas of life and ministry, but _____ _____ is the pattern. Pg. 56

_____

12. True or False? Any theology that makes Christ and His commands from primary focus is a heresy no matter how rejected its human source may be. Pg. 56

_____

13. It is not enough to be commissioned and sent out. What else is necessary? Pg. 56

_____

_____

14. What will require humility from ministries that are already established? Pg. 57

_____

_____

15. The Lord of the Harvest is sending conformed laborers into His harvest. What are these disciples conformed to? Pg. 57

_____

_____

16. What are the three elements that they author says are present in the command of Christ to His disciples found in Matthew 10? Pg. 57

_____

_____

17. Fill in the blanks: The Holy Spirit is at work creating the _____ of _____ _____ in believers. Pg. 57

_____

18. True or False? Every Christian ministry's goal should be to be increasing in His image and increasingly duplicating Christ's ministry. Pg. 57

_____

19. What two elements are found in these commands from Christ that have not been present in the other general statements about Christ's mass ministry found in previous chapters? Pg. 57

_____

_____

20. These two elements have not been present in the general statements. Where are they found? Pg. 57

21. What does Christ assume that His commissioned and instructed disciples will be able to do? Pg. 58

_____

_____

22. What had the Twelve received that they had to give? Pg. 58

_____

_____

23. What does Christ assume here about the disciples that might become an issue? Pg. 58

_____

_____

24. Fill in the blanks: Christ assumes a capacity in His disciples to _____ _____ healing and deliverance from evil spirits to others as a regular, on-going part of their ministry. Pg. 58

_____

25. True or False? Much modern theology treats healing as if it were a normal and expected expression of Christian ministry. Pg. 58

_____

26. What produces the ineffectiveness of some Christians in the ministry of healing, miracles and deliverance? Pg. 59

_____

_____

27. What is the "earlier failure" that the author describes? Pg. 59

_____

_____

28. What is a "serious disobedience" according to the author? Pg. 59

_____

_____

_____

29. In a passage found in Luke Chapter 10, Christ commands believers to pray that laborers would be sent into the plentiful harvest. What does the author says is a contrast with some modern teaching on prayer? Pg. 59

_____

_____

30. The author quotes a verse from "another place" to emphasize that the harvest is already prepared. Pg. 59-60

_____

_____

31. What will labors in the harvest need to be able to do consistently? Pg. 60

_____

_____

_____

_____

32. What does the author say is "intimately connected" with preaching the Gospel of the Kingdom? Pg. 60

_____

_____

33. When theology disputes that healing ministry is commanded for believers today, what are they disputing? Pg. 60

_____

_____

34. What does the author say is a "fact" about "everyone Christ sent"? Pg. 60

_____

_____

35. What must the Bride of Christ learn? Pg. 61

_____

_____

36. In a passage in Acts 4, the leadership of the Church was being threatened and responded with an interesting prayer. What did this prayer reveal? Pg. 61

_____

_____

37. How should believers speak the Word of God? Pg. 61

_____

_____

38. How did Peter and John expect that the risen Christ would validate the Gospel? Pg. 62

_____

_____

39. What should not escape the reader according to the author? Pg. 62

_____

_____

40. The author says that this suggests two things. What are they? Pg. 62

_____

_____

_____

_____

41. What were the Twelve going to do and what were they going to expect? Pg. 62

_____

_____

_____

_____

42. What do these verses in Acts 4:29-31 reveal about the disciples' beliefs and thoughts about healing? Pg. 62

_____

_____

_____

_____

43. The author writes that "there is nothing in this passage to suggest" what? Pg. 62

_____

_____

_____

_____

44. What did the disciples already know before they prayed in this situation and therefore did not need to seek God about? Pg. 62

_____

_____

45. How did the Twelve apostles come to already understand the Father's will on this matter of healing? Pg. 62

_____

_____

46. The author says that there is "no hint" of what? Pg. 62

_____

_____

47. The apostles simply asked the Father to do what three things in this prayer? Pg. 62

_____

_____

_____

_____

48. How does God respond to this prayer? What is the Father's unmistakable stamp of approval on this prayer? What does the Father grant? Pg. 62-63

_____

_____

_____

_____

49. Acts 5:12-16 records the results of the apostles speaking the word of God with boldness. What does this text reveal that continued powerfully through the apostles? Pg. 63

_____

_____

50. The text reveals that these miraculous events were happening at "the hands of the apostles". The author writes that this statement implies what about the nature of the events and the level of control of the apostles? Pg. 63

_____

_____

51. What attitude is challenged by the fact of there being many signs and wonders? Pg. 63

_____

_____

_____

_____

52. True or False: Signs and wonders were mysterious to the apostles and should be today. Pg. 63

_____

53. What was the "powerful, intended effect" beyond the obvious help that ill and injured people received? Pg. 64

_____

_____

54. Fill in the blank: Supernatural ministry was important in _____ then, and is still important today. Pg. 64

_____

55. What kind of atmosphere and momentum does supernatural ministry create and obtain? Pg. 64

_____

_____

_____

_____

56. The behavior of people in this passage reveals what? Pg. 64

57. What did God do in response to the growing faith of these people? Pg. 64

58. God healed some simply by Peter's shadow cross them. What is this similar to? Pg. 64

59. What does healing a number of sick people through the unusual means of Peter's shadow reveal? Pg. 64

60. What was the essential element in healing of these people? Pg. 64

61. True or False? This passage reveals that healing was not some sort of unexplainable, unpredictable or sovereign act of God. Pg. 64

62. This author says that this passage involving the ministry of the apostles is strongly reminiscent of what? Pg. 64

63. Luke says that "all were being healed" in this situation. How is Luke using the word "healed"? Pg. 64-65

64. What does Luke using "healed" in this way imply? What does this not suggest? Pg. 65

65. In the summary of the Twelve apostle's ministry, the author says that the miraculous and what are found together repeatedly? Pg. 65

66. In the second point in the summary, the author says that healing and what else are often found together in the ministry of the Twelve apostles? What is this like according to the author? Pg. 65

_____

_____

67. In the third point in the summary, the author says that the idea of "performing miracles" is repeatedly found in various passages describing the ministry of the Twelve. Where else is this expression found repeatedly? Pg. 65

_____

_____

68. The general accounts of the ministry of the Twelve apostles occasionally reveal what? What are they like to not address at all. Pg. 65

_____

_____

_____

_____

69. What do these general accounts in the ministry of the Twelve apostles never describe? What is this like according to the author? Pg. 65

_____

_____

70. Those that express the idea that it might not be God's will to heal someone are expressing what according to the author? Pg. 65

_____

_____

_____

_____

Chapter Five
Ministry to the Masses by
Stephen, Philip, Barnabus, & Paul

1. The author says that the description of Stephen's ministry in the book of Acts is reminiscent of what? Pg. 66

_____

_____

2. Fill in the blanks: Stephen was one of the seven _____ and had the distinction of being the first _____ of the Church. Pg. 66

_____

3. What did Stephen know about the Holy Spirit? Pg. 66

_____

_____

4. Fill in the blank: Another of the first seven deacons of the Church, Philip had the distinction of being the only _____ that the New Testament tells us about. Pg. 66

_____

5. What same triad of elements is found in the ministry of Philip? Pg. 67

_____

_____

6. The author says that anything less than the "triad" above will be somewhat less than what? Pg. 67

_____

_____

7. Why did Philip have the attention of the multitudes like Christ before him? Pg. 67

_____

_____

8. What seriously questions the idea that healing and miracles are mysterious and sovereign acts of God? Pg. 67

_____

_____

_____

9. The passage uses the word "sign" but reveals what these signs were exactly. What were they? Pg. 67-68

10. What kinds of conditions does the passage particularly point out as being healed? Pg. 68

_____

_____

11. Fill in the blank: The passage reveals that _____ were healed and delivered from unclean spirits? Pg. 68

_____

12. The Gospels and Acts do not draw strong distinctions between healing and deliverance from evil spirits. The writers of Scripture express the same attitudes toward both aspects of ministry. What does this strongly suggest? Pg. 68

_____

_____

_____

13. True or False? Christ, the Twelve apostles, Stephen and Philip treat demons and sickness in the same manner, always as an enemy. Pg. 68

_____

14. Christ, the Twelve apostles, Stephen and Philip never do what? Pg. 68

_____

_____

_____

15. What should anyone with "normal logic" see that Christ's supernatural ministry through His servants would produce? Pg. 68

_____

_____

16. On the other hand, what will religious teaching suggest? Pg. 68

_____

_____

_____

17. What will some who are confused by religious teaching do intuitively when they are sick? Pg. 68-69

_____

_____

_____

18. What does Christ consistently do as the true revelation of the Father's love? Pg. 69.

_____

_____

19. Who was Simon? Pg 69

_____

_____

20. While Simon had some serious character problems, he was also became what? Pg. 69

_____

_____

_____

21. What is absent from this account as in many other passages? Pg. 69

_____

_____

_____

22. In Acts 14:1-3, Paul and Barnabus also duplicated the ministry of Christ. The author notes that Paul and Barnabus were speaking boldly about Christ. The author says that this is a prerequisite for what? Pg. 69-70

_____

_____

23. Fill in the blanks: In this verse, the _____ _____ can be seen. On the human side of the equation, Barnabus and Paul who were _____ on the Lord. On the divine side of the equation was the risen Christ who was _____ _____ to the word of His grace. Pg. 70

_____

_____

24. Fill in the blanks: On the human side of the equation, Paul and Barnabus were_____ _____ the word of His grace. On the divine side of the equation, the risen Christ was bearing witness by _____ that signs and wonders be done by their hands. On the human side of the equation Paul and Barnabus' hands were_____ the signs and wonders. Pg. 70-71

_____

_____

25. A chapter later, in Acts 15:12, how is this divine balance again revealed? Pg. 71

_____

_____

26. True or False? Those who want to completely disconnect the power of God from human vessels do it without biblical license. Pg. 71

_____

_____

27. True or False? According to the author, those that want to emphasize the human side of the equation in the miraculous do it at the expense of the sovereignty of God seen clearly in the New Testament. Pg. 71

_____

28. What will happen if believers fail to see the human side of the equation? Pg. 71

_____

_____

29. The author says that a general passage in Romans 15:18-19 seems to sum up, in many respects, Paul's theology of the miraculous and what else? Pg. 71

_____

30. Paul's lack of hesitation (willingness) to do what would invite criticism today? Pg. 71-72

_____

_____

_____

_____

31.True or False? Modern attitudes towards healing and miracles are often in harmony with biblical values. Pg. 72

_____

32. What does the author say that the phrase "…what Christ has accomplished through me…" reveals again. Pg. 72

_____

_____

33. What was the result of Christ working through Paul? Pg. 72

_____

_____

34. What does the author speculate that the message that Paul was preaching was? ? Why? Pg. 72

_____

_____

35. What was responsible for Paul's success? Pg. 72

_____

_____

36. What is necessary to "fully preach the gospel of Christ"? Pg. 72

_____

_____

37. Fill in the blanks: Paul understood that the power of signs and wonders _____ _____ _____ was the only way to fully preach the gospel and to bring the _____ _____ of the Gentiles to _____ to Christ. Pg. 72

_____

38. Laborers in the harvest must be equipped to do what? Pg. 73

_____

_____

39. What affirmed the apostleship of the apostle Paul? Pg. 73

_____

_____

40. Paul reveals that believers should be able to distinguish a true apostle by what? Pg. 73

_____

_____

41. Why are alternative explanations of apostleship often given? Pg. 73

_____

_____

_____

_____

_____

42. True or False? The power to heal is limited to apostles. Pg. 73

_____

43. What two gifts are listed with seven other gifts that the Holy Spirit gives? Pg. 74

_____

_____

44. True or False? Paul does not show that one gift in particular is to be desired above the others. Pg. 74

_____

45. True or False? The gifts of healing and effecting of miracles require more faith and greater spirituality than the other gifts. Pg. 74

_____

46. How else is the phrase "effecting of miracles" translated? Pg. 74

_____

_____

47. Fill in the blank: The gift of working miracles is to _____ _____ ___ _____ Pg, 74

48. The very name of this gift reveals what? Pg. 74

_____

_____

_____

49. In 1 Corinthians 12:28, Paul reveals that some are appointed in the Church to do miracles and healing in the same way that some are appointed as what? Pg. 74

_____

_____

50. What has changed so that gifted individuals in local churches can learn how to function in supernatural giftings? Pg. 75

_____

_____

_____

_____

51. The final general description of the ministry of Christ's Disciples is found in Hebrews 2:3-4. The writer of Hebrews relates that the original witnesses of Christ confirmed the word of Christ to them. The author says this sound similar to what? Pg. 75-76

_____

_____

_____

_____

52. Who bore witness with the original hearers and how was that witness made? Pg. 76

_____

_____

_____

_____

53. What does the author say is clear concerning God's will? Pg. 76

_____

_____

_____

_____

Introduction to Specific Events

1. True or False? All the miracles and healing in Christ's ministry are described in detail by the writers of the four authors of the Gospel accounts. Pg. 78

_____

2. How many people does the author say were healed by observation of the general accounts of Christ's ministry to the masses. Pg. 78

_____

_____

3. What situation did the apostle John note at the end of his Gospel? Pg. 78

_____

_____

_____

_____

4. Why does the author believe that the Gospel of John records mostly different miracles and healings than the other Gospel writers? Pg. 78

_____

_____

_____

_____

5. True or False? When the apostle John wrote the Gospel of John there were many miracles and healings that no one had recorded. Pg. 79

_____

6. What was John's criteria in selection of the events that he records in his Gospel? Pg. 79

_____

_____

_____

_____

7. The author says that Luke was "obviously aware" of something. What was it? Pg. 80

_____

_____

_____

8. What two Gospels could Luke have been referring to? Pg. 80

_____

_____

9. Fill in the blank: Luke reminds us that_____ compiled these accounts. Pg. 80

10. What does the author believe was Luke's reasoning that another Gospel was needed? Pg. 80

_____

_____

_____

_____

11. What additional details and differences does Luke's Gospel offer? Pg. 80

_____

_____

_____

_____

_____

12. What does the name "Theophilus" mean? Why does this name potentially mean that there was not a specific person that Luke was addressing? Pg. 81

_____

_____

_____

_____

13. What does the author say was Luke's "real motive" for writing his Gospel? Pg. 81

_____

_____

14. True or False? Neither John, Mark nor Matthew reveals to their readers their motivations for writing their Gospels. Pg. 81

_____

15. The author suggests that the motives of all the writers of the Gospels were similar. What motive does he believe they had in writing their Gospels? Pg. 81

_____

_____

_____

16. How many specific healings or healing miracles are performed by Christ are recorded in the Gospels? Pg. 81

_____

_____

17. What guided the selection of particular miracles and healings? Pg. 82

_____

_____

18. True or False? Something special is revealed in each specific event in the Gospel's record. Pg. 82

_____

19. What do the Gospel writers often reveal within the specific accounts of miracles and healings? Pg. 82

_____

_____

20. What will studying these specific accounts reveal? Pg. 82

_____

_____

_____

_____

21. What does the author say that the next chapters of his book will seek to do? Pg. 82

_____

_____

22. What would be nearly impossible to present if it were not for the unique nature of three of the four Gospels? Pg. 82

_____

_____

_____

_____

23. Fill in the blanks: Because the Gospels of Matthew, Mark, and Luke have a clear relationship between them, they have been called the _____ _____. Pg. 82

_____

24. What does the term "Synoptic" mean? Pg. 82

_____

_____

25. What does the fact that many of the verses in the Synoptic Gospels (Matthew, Mark, and Luke) are nearly or exactly the same mean for the study in the book? Pg. 83

_____

_____

_____

26. How many specific miracles or healings in Christ's ministry are repeated in all three Gospels? Pg. 83

27. How many specific miracles or healings in Christ's ministry are repeated in two Gospels but not three? Pg. 83

_____

_____

28. How many specific miracles or healings in Christ's ministry are found only in one Gospel? Pg. 83

_____

_____

29. How many (total) distinctly different specific miracles and healing events are found in the four Gospels? Pg. 83

_____

_____

30. Why are some of the miracles in the life of Christ not included in this book? Pg. 83

_____

_____

31. What are some of the kinds of miracles that are not reviewed in this book? Pg. 83

_____

_____

_____

_____

32. How are the chapters following the Introduction to Christ's Specific Healings and Miracles organized? Pg. 83

_____

_____

_____

_____

33. Some healings could be placed in two chapters. What has the author done in such cases? Pg. 83

_____

_____

Chapter Six
Christ Heals the Blind

1. Christ healed two blind men in Matthew 9:27-31. When did this event happen in the life of Christ? Pg. 84

_____

_____

2. The author writes that this event "may be even clearer" on what important matter? Pg. 84

_____

_____

3. What is the meaning of "mercy" quoted from Vine's Dictionary? Pg. 84

_____

_____

_____

_____

4. By asking Christ for "mercy" what did these two blind men demonstrate? Pg. 84-85

_____

_____

5. How did these men identify Christ as the Jewish Messiah? Pg. 85

_____

_____

6. What reveals that Christ postponed ministry to these two blind men? Pg. 85

_____

_____

7. What "fact" reveals the determination of these blind men to be healed? Pg. 85

_____

_____

8. True or False? Christ was not actively seeking these blind men to heal them. Pg. 85

_____

9. True or False? These blind men initiated the discourse with Christ concerning their healing. Pg. 85

_____

10. What important question does Christ ask these blind men? Pg. 85

_____

_____

11. In a footnote at the bottom of page 85, the author reminds readers of what? Pg. 85

_____

_____

12. What is the "central issue" in the healing of these men according to the author? Pg. 85

_____

_____

13. How do these two blind men respond to this question? Pg. 86.

_____

_____

14. How does their answer reflect a submissive attitude? Pg. 86

_____

_____

15. What ordinary method of imparting healing did Christ use to heal them? Pg. 86

_____

_____

16. How many times does Christ mention faith or believing before He heals these blind men? Pg. 86

_____

_____

17. What does the author say is "noteworthy"? Pg. 86

_____

_____

18. What does Christ "already know" about this matter? Pg. 86

_____

_____

19. Fill in the blanks: The issue of these men being healed is not an issue of the _____ of the _____, it is an issue of their _____. Pg. 86

_____

20. Fill in the blank: Christ reveals that these two blind men are in _____ of the matter of their healing. Pg. 86

_____

21. How will these blind men receive from the Father? Pg. 86

_____

_____

22. What does this imply about them if they had not believed? Pg. 86

_____

_____

23. The author writes that this situation would have been a "great situation" to demonstrate something if God had so desired. What could have the Father demonstrated in this situation if He had wished to do so? Pg. 86

_____

_____

_____

_____

24. What "principle" is not demonstrated in this situation or any other like it in Scripture? Pg. 86

_____

_____

_____

_____

25. The author notes six things are "the same" in this passage. What are they? Pg. 86-87

_____

_____

_____

_____

26. What other biblical principle is revealed in the healing of both men in the same way? Pg. 87

_____

_____

27. Fill in the blanks: What the Father will do for one person, He will do for another if that person _____ _____ _____ _____. Pg. 87

_____

28. The author writes that many have understood this "no respecter" principle in matters such as the forgiveness of sins but have failed to do what? Pg. 87

_____

_____

29. True or False? These men had precipitated their healings by expressing faith through seeking Christ for healing. Pg. 87

_____

30. True or False? These men confessed their faith on Christ's questioning of them. Pg. 87

_____

31. True or False? Christ did not say that faith was important for their healing. Pg. 87

_____

_____

32. The healing of these two blind men found in Matthew's Gospel happens chronologically during what year of Christ's ministry? Pg. 87

_____

_____

33. The next healing of a blind person that the author discusses is the healing of the blind beggar Bartimaeus. What year of Christ's ministry does this healing happen? Pg. 87

_____

_____

34. This healing happens in Mark's Gospel just before what other event? Pg. 87

_____

_____

35. What is the only significant difference between Luke's account of this healing and Mark's account? Pg. 87

_____

_____

36. What does the author say is possible, even probable, about Bartimaeus and the healing of the two blind men? Pg. 120.

_____

_____

37. What does the author speculate that Bartimaeus could have said to himself in light of hearing about the two blind men who were healed by Christ? Pg. 87-88

_____

_____

38. The author sees this as another expression of the principle of "God is not a respecter of persons". In light of other people's faith and success, what should our reaction when we are in need? Pg. 88

_____

_____

_____

39. Fill in the blanks: The _____, _____, and _____ of Christ again reveal that the will of the Father is settled in matters of healing. The Father wants _____ _____. Pg. 88

_____

40. The author contrasts the story of the two blind men with the story of Bartimaeus. He notes that this story has detailed personal information about Bartimaeus. The author speculates that Matthew might have been "subtly informing" his readers of what? Pg. 88

_____
_____
_____
_____

41. How is the response of Bartimaeus similar to the two blind men? Pg. 88

_____
_____
_____
_____

42. True or False? The author thinks that Bartimaeus may have thought that since Christ had healed the other two men, he didn't need to do the same things to be healed. Pg. 89

_____

43. True or False? The author thinks that Bartimaeus might have thought that if Christ healed the other blind men on this basis, He would heal him (Bartimaeus) on the same basis. Pg. 89

_____

44. The crowd in this story tried to silence Bartimaeus as he cried out to Christ. How did Bartimaeus respond to this discouragement? Pg. 89

_____
_____

45. Bartimaeus showed some persistence in seeking Christ despite the discouragement of the crowd. How did the two blind men in the earlier story show persistence? Pg. 89

_____
_____

46. What would have happened if Bartimaeus had listened to the discouragement of the crowd? Pg. 89

_____
_____

47. What erroneous reasoning could have caused Bartimaeus to be passive and not cry out for Christ? Pg. 89

48. How was Bartimaeus' persistence in crying out to Christ rewarded? Pg. 89

_____

_____

49. After Christ calls Bartimaeus, he cast aside his cloak. What does the author think that this action reveals about Bartimaeus' focus? Pg. 90

_____

_____

50. True or False? Bartimaeus is a good example of someone who was extremely careful, cautious and conservative being rewarded for his wisdom. Pg. 90

_____

_____

51. Fill in the blanks: Bartimaeus was _____ _____ to his healing. Pg. 90

_____

52. True or False? Bartimaeus expressed no doubt about the will of the God in his healing. Pg. 90

_____

53. The author writes that Christ does not have a chance to do something. What is that something? Pg. 90

_____

_____

54. Neither Christ nor Bartimaeus questions God on what matter? Pg. 90

_____

_____

55. Fill in the blanks: Without any _____ or _____, Christ tells Bartimaeus that his faith has made him well. Pg. 90

_____

56. The author writes that the elements of this story strong contradict and challenge what ideas? Pg. 90

_____

_____

_____

_____

57. What would have happened if Bartimaeus had believed the above ideas? Pg. 90-91

58. What concept did Bartimaeus grasp that was demonstrated in his persistence, determined focus, and strong commitment? Pg. 91

59. What kind of doctrine produces passivity in people? Pg. 91

60. True or False? The author writes that passive attitudes are seldom rewarded in Scripture. Pg. 91

61. Fill in the blanks: Much encouragement in found throughout the Bible to _____ _____ _____ for that which He alone can provide. Pg. 91

62. What will the Holy Spirit do for anyone actively seeking God for healing? Pg. 91

63. The next healing of a blind person in this book is Bethsaida's blind man. This healing is found in Mark 8:22-26. The author writes that this healing allows for an unusual possibility. What possibility is he referring to? Pg. 91

64. What caused people to bring the sick, the injured, the blind and the lame to Christ? Pg. 91

65. Why did people bring this man to Christ according to the passage? Pg. 91-92

66. Is the reason why Christ took this man out of the village of Bethsaida revealed in the passage? Pg. 92

_____

_____

67. How did Christ describe and compare Bethsaida in other passages such as Mark 11:20-21? Pg. 92

_____

_____

_____

_____

68. What two unusual and very public miracles occurred near Bethsaida? Pg. 92

_____

_____

69. The eyewitnesses to Christ's many miracles in this region should have done what? Did they do this? Pg. 92

_____

_____

70. The author speculates from the information about Bethsaida the possible reason that Christ took this blind man out of Bethsaida. What was that possible reason? Pg. 92-93

_____

_____

_____

_____

71. Fill in the blanks: Perhaps, the blind man's faith was _____ and _____. In any case, Christ created _____ for the blind man before He ministered to him. Pg. 93

_____

72. How many healing events using spittle in some way are recorded in the Gospels? Pg. 93

_____

_____

73. Did every healing event in Christ's ministry require an unusual methodology? Pg. 93

_____

_____

74. True or False? Healings or miracles always require a word of knowledge so that the one praying will know what kind of methodology to use. Pg. 93

_____

75. The author points out that Christ also used a "normal method" in this situation which is also Christ's "ongoing method of choice"? What was it? Pg. 93

_____

_____

76. While Christ did not need specific guidance to do this healing, He maintained openness to what? Pg. 93

_____

_____

77. What does Christ's question "Do you see anything?" reveal? Pg. 93-94

_____

_____

78. The author says that while there is no mystery in the Father's will, what may be a surprise? Pg. 94

_____

_____

79. What are some of the manifestations that people may feel when they are being healed? Pg. 94

_____

_____

_____

_____

80. If someone receives a partial healing, how should that encourage them? Pg. 94

_____

_____

81. How did the man respond to Christ's question? Pg. 94

_____

_____

82. True or False: Instantaneous healing is not the only expression of Christ's healing ministry. Pg. 94

_____

83. What ought to be the final result when a partial healing is received? Pg. 94

_____

_____

84. The author writes about "sanctified logic" motivating a believer to receive a complete healing. What is this "sanctified logic"? Pg. 94

_____

85. Fill in the blanks: Christ did not _____ for a partial healing. Christ knew that the Father's will was complete wholeness _____ _____ _____ the man received healing. Pg. 94

_____

_____

86. Fill in the blanks: For someone to have an _____ ministry that models itself on _____ _____, allowance must be made for an occasional situation like this. In a very few cases, _____ a person _____ _____ _____ may be the only way to get them healed. Pg. 95

_____

_____

87. How long was the interval between the partial healing and the man's complete healing? Pg. 95

_____

_____

88. What must anyone wishing to accomplish healing like the Savior be willing to do? Pg. 95

_____

_____

89. What were Christ's final instructions to the man? Pg. 95

_____

_____

90. The next event of a blind person being healed is the man born blind found in John Chapter 9. This is the only specifically mentioned case of what? Pg. 96

_____

_____

91. Why is this story very important according to the author? Pg. 96

_____

_____

92. What other issue appears in the story? Pg. 96

_____

_____

93. The text says that Christ "saw" this man. What does the author conclude about Christ's behavior from the question that the disciples asked Christ about the man? Pg. 96

_____

94. What assumption do the disciples make that is implicit in the question? Pg. 97

_____

_____

95. The author states that the logic of the man's sins being the cause of his blindness is weak. How does the author come to this conclusion? Pg. 97

_____

_____

96. The author states that the logic of a child being punished for the parent's sins is not much better. However, the author does say that this is a possibility for what scriptural reason? Pg. 97

_____

_____

_____

_____

97. Does the author think that Christ's answer in this case validates the possibility that the sins of the parents were the cause. Pg. 97

_____

_____

98. What does Christ make clear about sin in this case? Pg. 97

_____

_____

99. What is the "blame game"? Pg. 97

_____

_____

100. How does the "blame game" affect the healing and deliverance of people? Pg. 97

_____

_____

101. True or False? Christ normally healed people without saying a word about their sins or what caused their sickness and without fixing blame. Pg. 97

_____

102. True or False? In Christ's public preaching of the Kingdom of God, repentance was an important part. Pg. 97

_____

103. True or False? Christ public ministry called people to repentance, but in His ongoing ministry to individuals, He seldom said anything about their need to repent. Pg. 97-98

_____

104. Who are the three kinds of persons blamed for sickness or disability. Pg. 98

_____

_____

105. Fill in the blanks: Blame is most often fixed on _____. This is often very _____ and _____ with _____. Pg. 98

_____

106. Fill in the blanks: This hidden blame is _____ _____, and sickness and debilitating conditions are _____ into a _____ _____ from the Father. Pg. 98

_____

107. What is difficult for someone who loses a child to a sickness or suffers a debilitating and painful condition? Pg. 98

_____

_____

108. What is the first of two logical arguments that sometimes are used to give God the responsibility for the loss? Pg. 98

_____

_____

_____

_____

109. What does this logic overlook? Pg. 98

_____

_____

_____

_____

110. What is the second of two logical arguments that sometimes are used to give God the responsibility for the loss? Pg. 98

_____

_____

_____

111. What does this logic forget? Pg. 98

_____

_____

112. What is often hidden in people wounded by such painful circumstances? Pg. 98

_____

_____

113. What kind of problems do these people have after being wounded by such circumstances? Pg. 98

_____

_____

114. True or False: The author writes that God is good despite the fact that He is the source of their pain. Pg. 98-99

_____

115. Instead of fixing blame on anyone what should we do according to the author? Pg. 99

_____

_____

116. What does Christ reveal about why this man had this condition? Pg. 99

_____

_____

117. Did the man's blindness bring God any glory before He was healed? Pg. 99

_____

_____

118. True or False: This man's disability brought God glory. Pg. 99

_____

119. Why was this man's healing so powerful a testimony? Pg. 99

_____

_____

120. Why should no one ever wait to be healed? Pg. 99

_____

_____

121. Does the length of time that a person has a particular condition reveal that that condition is the will of the Father for them? How can we know this from the life of Christ? Pg. 100

_____

_____

_____

122. What did the Father want from the beginning for these people with long-term conditions? Pg. 100

_____

_____

123. The author says that there is clear encouragement in this passage from Christ to the disciples to do the same kinds of miraculous works as healing the blind man. What was that encouragement? Pg. 100

_____

_____

124. What was the work of the Father in this passage? Pg. 100

_____

_____

125. Fill in the blanks: Nothing in this passage indicates that the work of the Father was happening _____ this man's healing. Nothing in this passage reveals that some _____ _____ of the Father was happening in this man by virtue of his condition of blindness. Pg. 100

_____

126. Fill in the blanks: The phrase "We must work the works of the Father" reveals the _____ _____ _____in healing and miracle ministry. While these are the Father's works, _____ must work them. Pg. 101

_____

127. True or False? God's preferred way is to heal without using a human vessel. Pg. 101

_____

128. In the New Testament, it is unusual for someone to be healed in what way? Pg. 101

_____

_____

129. If opportunity still exists, then what should believers being doing? Pg. 101

_____

_____

130. How do believers become "the light of the world"? Pg. 101

_____

_____

131. What practical concern that might have helped the man's faith that might have prompted Christ to apply clay to the eyes of this blind man? Pg. 101-102

_____

_____

_____

_____

132. What other practical concern might have prompted Christ to have the man go to the pool of Siloam? Pg. 102

_____

_____

_____

133. How did the man demonstrate that he had faith to be healed? Pg. 102

_____

_____

_____

134. Why does this chapter come early in the specific events of Christ's healing ministry? Pg. 102

_____

_____

135. Why does the author say that this belief is unfortunate? Pg. 102

_____

_____

_____

136. Fill in the blanks: Believers have _____ _____ in _____, without _____, to heal anyone of anything. Pg. 102

_____

137. Fill in the blanks: One thing is _____ _____than another. Pg. 102

_____

138. Fill in the blanks: Believers must understand that _____ _____ _____ them despite their _____ and feelings of _____. Pg. 102

_____

139. Christ is capable and willing to do mighty things through what? Pg. 102

_____

_____

Chapter Seven
Christ Heals Infections and Fevers

1. The first incident that this chapter deals with is the cleansing of the ten lepers found in Luke 17:12-19. Why did these leprous men stand at a distance from Christ? Pg. 103

_____

_____

_____

_____

2. What did people believe about lepers? Pg. 104

_____

_____

3. What did living outside the camp of the healthy mean for the lives of lepers? Pg. 104

_____

_____

4. What causes lepers to lose their fingers, toes or portions of their faces? Pg. 104

_____

_____

_____

_____

5. What causes fear in the uninfected? Pg. 105

_____

_____

_____

_____

6. Sometimes leprosy was a judgement of God in the Old Testament. What other more modern disease has been seen as a judgement of God? Pg. 105

_____

_____

7. Are people who are infected with leprosy or AIDS always responsible for contracting their illness? Pg. 105

_____

_____

8. Does Christ deal with people who are responsible for their illness differently than those who are not responsible? Pg. 105

_____

_____

9. What was Christ's instructions to these lepers? Pg. 105

_____

_____

10. What did priests and the Law of Moses have to do with infectious illness? Pg. 105

_____

_____

11. Fill in the blanks: If the lepers had not_____ that they were _____, they would have not left the _____ of _____. Pg. 105

_____

_____

12. Fill in the blanks: Their faith in resulted in_____ to His _____. Their _____ of _____ resulted in their healing. Pg. 106

_____

13. The author says that this would have been "an ideal opportunity" for the Holy Spirit to demonstrate what? What was actually demonstrated? Pg. 106

_____

_____

_____

_____

14. The New Testament has a specific English word connected to the healing of leprosy. What is it? Pg. 106

_____

_____

15. What is the Greek word that is translated into the English word above? How is this word defined? Pg. 106

_____

_____

16. The healing of leprosy was to purify, to purge, to make the leprous person spotless and clean in a physical and what other sense? Pg. 106

_____

_____

17. What do the four physical reactions of the man who returned to give thanks reflect? Pg. 106

_____

_____

18. According to the author, this man saw something in Christ that the other nine did not see. What did he see? Pg. 107

19. Christ's surprised reaction to the nine who did not return tells us that they obviously failed to react properly. Christ's surprise also reveals what other important fact? Pg. 107

_____

_____

20. What truth did the man who returned get to hear that the other nine did not? Pg. 107

_____

_____

21. What two things does the healing of other nine lepers reveal about the graciousness and mercy of God? Pg. 108

_____

_____

_____

_____

_____

_____

22. The second account of a healing of a leper covered in this chapter is found in Matthew 8:1-4. This man could have been what person named elsewhere in the Gospels? Pg. 108

_____

_____

23. This healing occurs right after what important discourse? Pg. 109

_____

_____

24. The leper acknowledges what when he called Christ "Lord"? Pg. 109

_____

_____

25. What "emotional and spiritual place" has this leper come to that is the same as many people today? What is he not entirely sure about? Pg. 109

_____

_____

_____

_____

26. The author says that much modern theology has taught these theological doubts rather than what? Pg. 109

27. This is the only place in the New Testament where the question of what is addressed in a direct way? Pg. 109

_____

_____

28. True or False? *Christ's reaction to this man ought to instruct believers about what the Father's will is in such matters.* Pg. 109-110

_____

29. Fill in the blanks: In this situation, Christ does not _____. Christ does not _____ to understand the Father's will in this circumstance. Christ _____ _____ the will of the Father in these matters. Pg. 110

_____

30. Christ does not give this man a theological dissertation about the will of God but rather His verbal expression comes from what? Pg. 110

_____

_____

31. Fill in the blanks: Much modern theology produces _____ _____ and _____ reactions to the sick or injured people that limit _____ and _____ for healing. Pg. 110

_____

32. Fill in the blanks: This theology produces _____ that the person will be spiritually _____ by possible failure in _____ God for healing. Pg. 110

_____

33. The author states that those embracing this theology somehow think what? Pg. 110

_____

_____

34. What is the illogical behavior found with this complex theology? Pg. 110

_____

_____

_____

35. If they actually believed that the injury, sickness or suffering was the will of God, and therefore doing some mysterious good, they would not do what? Pg. 110

_____

_____

36. Fill in the blanks: This theology produces _____ that seeking God for healing will ruin some _____ _____ from God that they are willing to ruin themselves by _____ a _____. Pg. 110-111

_____

37. Christ did not have a complex emotional and theological reaction to this man. How did He react? Pg. 111

_____

_____

38. The author points out that Christ's reaction after the man was healed is rather different than many modern expressions of ministry. In what way is it different? Pg. 111

_____

_____

_____

_____

39. The author says that the motive for a believer going back to the doctor after being healed would not be doubt or fear but what? Pg. 111

_____

_____

40. The third account of a healing of an infection is found in John 4:46-48. This story concerns a royal official that may have been a relative or ally of who? Pg. 112

_____

_____

41. What were the relatives/allies of King Herod called as a class of people? What were they like? Pg. 112

_____

_____

_____

_____

42. What motivated the royal official to seek out Christ in this situation? Pg. 112

_____

_____

_____

_____

43. Christ's response to this man is different than his response to other parents with sick children. What does Christ's response show? What do Christ's words and tone reveal? Pg. 112

_____

_____

_____

_____

44. Christ reproves an unspecified "you people" for "failure to believe". Who is Christ reproving by saying this? Pg. 112

_____

_____

45. The author writes that Christ is obviously not doing something when He makes this statement. What is Christ not doing when He said this? Pg. 112.

_____

_____

46. How did the royal official react to Christ's correction? Pg. 112

_____

_____

47. Fill in the blanks: _____ is not faith. Faith is not based on _____. Pg. 113

_____

48. The author thinks that something was possibly different after this man received Christ's correction. What was different? Pg. 113

_____

_____

49. The author thinks that at the moment that the man started believing something transpired. What happened? Pg. 113

_____

_____

_____

_____

_____

_____

50. The author says that it seems that Christ was reporting what fact about this healing? Pg. 113-114

_____

_____

51. When the royal official returned home what did he discover about the timing of his son's recovery? Pg. 114

_____

_____

52. What does "precise timing" often demonstrate? Pg. 114

_____

_____

53. What does the Greek word that is translated "fever" in this passage come from? What does it mean? Pg. 114

_____

_____

54. Fill in the blanks: Because of the _____ _____ in _____ as _____ a remarkable miracle happened, the fever left at the _____ _____ that Christ told the father that the child was well at some distance away. Pg. 114

_____

55. How many times is believing mentioned in this account of healing? Pg. 114

_____

_____

56. What does the apostle John call this miracle? Pg. 115

_____

_____

57. John also says that "Jesus performed" this sign. What does this imply? Pg. 115

_____

_____

58. Christ healed the mother-in-law of Peter in Luke 4:38-39. When did this happen in His ministry? Pg. 115

_____

_____

59. How did physicians classify fevers in Christ's day? What kind of fever did Peter's mother-in-law have according to the physician Luke? Pg. 115-116

_____

_____

_____

_____

60. The author says that Luke is extraordinarily precise in how he words these accounts. Since Luke says that "Christ rebuked the fever" and "it left her", what does this hint at according to the author? Pg. 116

_____

_____

Chapter Eight
Healing and Demonic Activity

1. The author covers deliverance ministry in a general way in the first five pages of this chapter. After that this chapter will be limited to what? Pg. 117

_____

_____

_____

_____

2. The author writes that something has happened in the past thirty years. What has happened? Pg. 117

_____

_____

3. How is this increase of those ministering deliverance related to the Second Coming of Christ? Pg. 117

_____

_____

_____

_____

4. What happens when there is no deliverance ministry in churches? What does not having deliverance ministry create in the life of the Church? Pg. 117

_____

_____

_____

_____

5. What eventually happens because there seems to be no solution to the problems of believers? Pg. 117

_____

_____

6. Fill in the blanks: If _____ is for today, then _____ _____ _____ is for today. Pg. 118

_____

7. Fill in the blanks: Where there is_____ _____ in Christ operating, then we would expect to see this _____. Pg. 118

_____

8. Fill in the blanks: Where these signs _____ to _____ there must be a _____ _____ that is usually a result of _____ _____ on these matters. Pg. 118

9. Fill in the blanks: Deliverance ministry is one aspect of the _____ _____ that Jesus purchased at _____ _____. Pg. 119

10. The Greek word translated "saved" is "sozo". This Greek word is translated in what other ways? Pg. 119

11. True or False? Salvation is healing and deliverance from evil spirits as well as being saved from hell. Pg. 119

12. Fill in the blanks: Deliverance is received by _____ just like _____ from sin, the _____ in the Holy Spirit or _____. Pg. 119

13. Fill in the blanks: Not all Christians are _____ _____, in all aspects, what Christ did for them on the cross. Pg. 119

14. What do believers fail to appropriate these provisions of salvation? Pg. 119

15. How do believers apply the defeat of the enemy? Pg. 119

16. Fill in the blanks: Deliverance ministry is normally for Christians. This means that many who need deliverance are _____ _____ _____ by demonic power. Pg. 119

17. True or False? A few people need extensive deliverance but most believers may only need a little. Pg. 120

18. The author states that the use of the words "possessed", "obsessed" and "oppressed" in translation are unfortunate. What word or phrase would be closer to the meaning of the verb "diamonizominoi"? Pg. 120

_____

19. The actual Greek verb does not imply two things. What are they? Pg. 121

_____

_____

_____

_____

20. What results when a Christian is demonized? Pg. 121

_____

_____

21. Fill in the blanks: Since God owns the Christian, a demon is an _____ _____ on God's property. This _____ _____ is _____ _____ by the exercise of _____ _____ of believers in the name of Jesus. Pg. 121

_____

22. The first specific event of healing through deliverance ministry is found in Matthew 17:14-17. This situation is compared and contrasted with what other event? Pg. 122

_____

_____

23. What would a literal translation of the Greek word describing the boy's condition be? Pg. 122

_____

_____

24. The boy's condition is misdiagnosed. What is the real cause of his condition? Why is this condition dangerous? Pg. 122

_____

_____

25. This boy's condition has often been thought to be what? Pg. 122

_____

_____

_____

_____

26. Christ has a strong reaction to His disciples' failure to help the boy. What does Christ say in reaction? Pg. 123

_____

_____

27. The author points out that the Greek word translated "perverted" means what literally? Pg. 123

_____

_____

28. Why couldn't the disciples deal with this situation? Pg. 123

_____

_____

_____

_____

29. What is not an obstacle affecting this child's healing? Pg. 123

_____

_____

30. What is the obstacle to the healing that is revealed in this passage? Pg. 123

_____

_____

_____

_____

31. The disciples ask Christ "Why could we not cast it out?" Had these men cast out demons before? Pg. 124

_____

_____

32. How does Christ answer their question? Why had they failed to deal with the boy's need? Pg. 124

_____

_____

33. Christ uses the mustard seed to illustrate faith. What was Christ trying to illustrate by using this very small object? Pg. 124

_____

_____

34. Fill in the blanks: A microscopically small amount of faith will cause _____ to be _____ to them. Humanly _____ _____ that would become possible would be the healing and deliverance of people with _____ _____, _____, and _____. Pg. 124

_____

35. What was the cause of the partial "failure" in the situation in Christ's hometown where He was unable to do miracles and only able to heal a few people? Pg. 125

_____

_____

36. What is a textual variant? Pg. 125

_____

_____

37. What does this textual variant indicate about the strength of some demons? Pg. 125

_____

_____

38. The author says that greater faith in Christ is easily obtainable. What is needed in an unusually difficult situation like this one? Pg. 125

_____

_____

_____

_____

39. In the account of the Gerasene Demoniac found in Luke 8:27-36, why is the man insane? Pg. 126

_____

_____

40. What are some of the specific details about this man that the account gives us? Pg. 126

_____

_____

41. How did the man react to Christ's presence? Pg. 127

_____

_____

42. True or False: In the beginning of this story, it seems that Christ is dealing with many demons. Pg. 127

_____

_____

43. When the complete context of the conversation with the man is considered, what conclusion about who is speaking can be made? Pg. 127

_____

_____

44. What do the demons know about Christ? What does their question to Christ reveal? Pg. 127

_____
_____
_____
_____
_____
_____

45. How was Christ tormenting the demons? Pg. 127

_____
_____

46. Fill in the blanks: Christ had commanded the spirits to come out of the man without _____. The unclean spirits remained in this man _____ Christ had commanded them to come out. Pg. 127

_____

47. True or False? This is another place where Christ worked with someone through a spiritual need until they were healed or delivered. Pg. 127

_____

48. True or False? If one has a Christ-like ministry, then everything must occur the first time you pray. Pg. 127-128

_____

49. Fill in the blanks: The way that a portion of the text reads indicates that there were _____ of _____ for this man when _____ _____ was not entirely obvious. Pg. 128

_____

50. The attempts to restrain the man reveals what kind of concerns? Pg. 128

_____
_____

51. Demons would drive this man into the desert. Mark adds a small but important detail about the bizarre behavior of the man. What is this detail? Pg. 128

_____
_____

52. The man's ability to break free from chains, shackles and guards reveals what? Pg. 128

_____
_____

53. What does Christ assume about the demon(s) that He questions? Pg. 129

_____

_____

54. What did the demons know that Christ could do to them? What did they attempt to do as a result of this knowledge? Pg. 129

_____

_____

_____

_____

55. What were the demons particularly distressed over? Pg. 129

_____

_____

56. True or False? Christ fulfills the demons' request by allowing them to enter a herd of swine. Pg. 129

_____

57. The author speculates on why Christ allowed the demons to enter the swine. What does he think? Pg. 129-130

_____

_____

_____

_____

58. Fill in the blanks: The man was in his _____ _____ as a result of the demons leaving him. Pg. 130

_____

59. This man had been "made well". The Greek word found here translated as "made well" could also be translated in what ways? Pg. 130

_____

_____

_____

_____

60. Fill in the blanks: This demonized and insane man experienced _____ in the form of _____ from evil spirits. Pg. 130

_____

61. The next event covered by the book is the healing of the blind and mute man found in Matthew 12:22-24. Demonic activity in this situation was causing what? Pg. 130

_____

_____

62. What does the author write is "unlikely" that "anyone knew"? Pg. 131

_____

_____

63. When did they come to know the true sources of this man's problems probably? Pg. 131

_____

_____

64. What would be possible today if someone was ignorant of the actual cause of a blind or mute person's disability was demonic activity? Pg. 131

_____

_____

_____

_____

65. Fill in the blanks: God is sometimes given credit for doing a _____ work for _____ in a person's disabilities when actually a _____ _____ work of _____ is taking place. Pg. 131

_____

66. How did this man get to Christ probably? Pg. 131

_____

_____

_____

_____

67. Fill in the blanks: Often the words for _____ are applied in the New Testament when _____ occurs from _____ _____ causing a condition or sickness. Pg. 132

_____

68. True or False? Any teaching on healing is incomplete if that teaching fails to deal with demonic activity producing sickness and disability. Pg. 132

_____

69. What was the effect of this deliverance healing on the masses? Pg. 132

_____

_____

_____

_____

70. How do miracles affect evangelism? Pg. 132

_____
_____
_____
_____

71. Who will not believe despite miracles at the end of the age? Pg. 132

_____
_____
_____
_____

72. The next event in the book is the Syro-Phoenician woman's daughter found in Matthew 15:21-28. Why does the author include this story? Pg. 133

_____
_____
_____
_____

73. This story takes place just after what event? How does that explain why the passage says that Christ "withdrew" into this area? What does the author suggest that He and His disciples were doing there? Pg. 133

_____
_____
_____
_____

74. How is the Canaanite (Syro-Phoenician) woman described in this passage? How does she address Christ and what does she ask for? Pg. 133

_____
_____
_____
_____

75. How is Christ's reaction to this woman different than some of the other descriptions of His healing ministry? Pg. 134

_____
_____

76. Why did the disciples ask Christ to do something about this woman? Pg. 134

_____
_____
_____
_____

77. Why didn't Christ initially help this woman? Pg. 134

_____

_____

_____

_____

78. "More than anything else" what is revealed in the passage about this woman? Pg. 134

_____

_____

79. How did Christ describe His ministry to this woman? Pg. 134

_____

_____

80. True or False? Christ suggested to this woman that responding to her needs would be a potential misuse of the spiritual resources that God had given Him. Pg. 135

_____

81. Fill in the blanks: She uses _____ own _____ and _____ to say that, even if there are _____ to Christ's ministry, there is such an _____ of bread that some is likely to end up as _____ that will feed the dogs. Pg. 135

_____

82. How does Christ see this woman's persistence? Pg. 135

_____

_____

83. Fill in the blanks: Despite Christ's _____ _____ for her cries, and His _____ explaining to her why He would not help her, she _____ and _____ what she wished from the Father. Her daughter was healed. Pg. 135

_____

84. True or False? Great faith allowed this woman to receive something that she was entitled to because of living in Israel. Pg. 136

_____

85. The next story in this chapter is the mute demoniac found in Matthew 9:32-34. What was causing this man to be mute? Pg. 136

_____

_____

86. Why would someone bring this man to Christ? Pg. 136

_____

_____

87. What were the two opposing reactions to this man's deliverance? Pg. 137

_____
_____
_____
_____
_____
_____

88. How is this like reactions today? Pg. 137

_____
_____
_____
_____
_____
_____

89. The next event in the book is the woman bound for eighteen years found in Luke 13:10-13. What symptom was the demon producing in this woman's life? Pg. 137

_____
_____

90. Did the woman or anyone else understand that an evil spirit was causing her problem? Pg. 138

_____
_____

91. Fill in the blanks: Deliverance needs may be _____ behind _____ _____ of disease or conditions. Pg. 138

_____

92. Fill in the blanks: Many people fail to recognize _____ _____ because they think that the person must be _____ _____ by _____ in order to need _____. Pg. 138

_____

93. What method did Christ use to heal this woman? Pg. 138

_____
_____

94. Many times laying hands on a person will produce a deliverance without what? Pg. 138

_____
_____

95. How does Christ's language indicate that a deliverance and not just a healing took place in this situation? Pg. 138-139

_____

_____

_____

_____

96. How did the leader of the Synagogue react to this deliverance? Pg. 139

_____

_____

_____

_____

97. How do some misguided religious leaders treat those who heal the sick today? Pg. 139

_____

_____

98. From the perspective of the onlookers, what did this deliverance appear to be? Was the demon evident to those who saw the event? Pg. 139-140

_____

_____

_____

_____

99. How did Christ answer the accusation of the synagogue leader that He had done something wrong by helping this woman? What logic does He argue? Pg. 140

_____

_____

_____

_____

_____

_____

100. What powerful truth emerges from Christ's comparison about "normal care for a believer"? Pg. 140

_____

_____

_____

_____

101. How could have Christ avoided criticism in this situation? Did He avoid criticism? Pg. 140

_____

_____

102. Why did Christ credit Satan with causing this woman's sickness when it was not Satan Himself but one of his subordinate spirits? Pg. 140-141

_____

_____

_____

_____

103. Fill in the blanks: Christ said that the eighteen years that this woman suffered were eighteen _____ years. Christ described what she experienced as being _____ from this _____. Pg. 141

_____

104. What might a person afflicted by the power of an evil spirit be taught today about their suffering? Pg. 141

_____

_____

_____

_____

105. What does misdiagnosis of the actual cause of conditions create? Pg. 141

_____

_____

106. What did the common people, the multitude, see Christ's ministry full of? Pg. 141

_____

_____

107. On the other hand, what was happening to the religious leaders? Pg. 141

_____

_____

108. Fill in the blanks: When leaders fail to humbly _____ themselves in the _____ arena, they may ultimately _____ out of _____ and _____ of those who are _____. Pg. 141-142

_____

109. In a passage in Luke 8:2-3, the author says that it is both general and specific. Why? Pg. 142

_____

_____

_____

_____

110. Luke's usage of "healed of evil spirits" in this passage may indicate what? Pg. 142

_____

_____

111. Because Luke has separated "evil spirits" from "sickness", this substantiates what fact? Pg. 142

_____

_____

112. The book's analysis of various passages concerning healing reveals the work of demons in sickness in some cases. What proportion of all the specific passages openly reveal demons causing the sickness or condition? Pg. 142

_____

_____

_____

_____

113. True or False? Any ministry wishing to function as Christ did in bringing healing ministry to people must be willing and able to deal with demonic activity when it is discovered. Pg. 142

_____

Chapter Nine
Christ Heals Disability & Injury

1. The first account of healing of a disability concerns the deaf and mute man in Decapolis found in Mark 7:32-37. What does this healing not mention that was seen in the previous chapter? Pg. 143

_____

_____

2. How does this situation reveal that Christ's most often used method of healing was the "laying on of hands"? Pg. 143-144

_____

_____

3. Christ changed the location of someone before healing them. In this case, the author suggests that since the healing of hearing was involved that Christ needed what? Pg. 144

_____

_____

_____

_____

4. Fill in the blank: Putting fingers into a deaf person's ears is a form of the _____ on of _____. Pg. 144

_____

5. What does the author say about the command for the ears to open? Pg. 145

_____

_____

_____

_____

6. What does the phrase "looking up to heaven with a deep sigh" suggest about the unusual methodology of using saliva? Pg. 144

_____

_____

7. What does the phrase "his ears were opened" imply about his condition before meeting Christ? Pg. 145

_____

_____

8. What does the word "impediment" mean from the literal Greek? Pg. 145.

9. What is the possible reason that Christ did not want anyone to publicize this miracle? Pg. 145

_____

_____

10. The disciples had observed Christ's ministry to all kinds of people with all kinds of problems. What was their testimony of His ministry? Pg. 145

_____

_____

11. What does the fact that the disciples knew that Christ had "done all things well" in the arena of healing suggest? Pg. 145

_____

_____

12. The author discusses a "theological loophole" were some have suggested that Christ did not heal everyone who came to Him in faith. If this were true what would it mean? How would it affect faith in Christ as Healer? Pg. 146

_____

_____

_____

_____

13. What does the author say is "impossible"? Pg. 146

_____

_____

14. Fill in the blanks: Believers can only have _____ in that which is _____ to be _____ _____. Pg. 146

_____

15. The next event of healing in this chapter is the man at the Sheep Gate pool. It is found in John Chapter 5. Does any other Gospel record this healing? Pg. 147

_____

_____

16. What does "Bethesda" mean in Hebrew? Pg. 147

_____

_____

17. Why were there a great number of sick and injured people waiting around this pool? Pg. 147

18. There is a verse in this account that is sometimes placed in parenthesis or not included at all except in margin notes or footnotes. Why? Pg. 148

_____

_____

_____

19. Other than the reason above, some have discounted this verse for some other reasons. What are they? Pg. 148

_____

_____

20. The author suggests that there is "no reason to doubt that this angelic phenomenon was actually happening" and offers some logic as well. On what basis does he believe this? Pg. 148

_____

_____

_____

21. What does the sick man himself confirm that is in all the manuscripts that seems to make the earlier textual variant verse valid? Pg. 148

_____

_____

22. What does Christ's question to the man suggest about the man's emotional condition? Pg. 148

_____

_____

23. What does the fact of this man being sick for thirty-eight years not reveal? Pg. 149

_____

_____

24. What could have discouraged this man? What does he seem to complain about? Pg. 149

_____

_____

_____

25. The author suggests that the man's faith might have been regenerated by Christ's question. Why? Pg. 149

26. Why does the author say that this healing is extremely encouraging? Pg. 150

_____

_____

_____

_____

27. True or False? The author states that sometimes people are healed that do not seem to meet the normal conditions of faith for healing. Pg. 150

_____

28. Fill in the Blanks: It seems that a kind of _____ _____ may receive healing if the person praying for them _____. However, the _____ of a possible recipient of healing seem to _____ the _____ of the person praying for them. Pg. 150

_____

29. What did Christ warn this man about later in the Temple? Pg. 150

_____

_____

30. The author writes it is likely that Christ was telling the man what? Pg. 150

_____

_____

31. What does the fact that Christ does not address the man's need for forgiveness suggest? Pg. 150-151

_____

_____

32. What have some pointed out about this healing? What does this seem like proof of for these people? Pg. 151

_____

_____

_____

_____

33. The author says that this is a misunderstanding of Christ's ministry since Christ did not heal every sick person in every city that He ministered in. In fact, in those passages where it says Christ "healed all" what are those texts referring to? Pg. 151

_____

_____

34. Those who came to Christ for healing were demonstrating what? Pg. 151

_____
_____

35. What were those who did not come demonstrating? Pg. 151

_____
_____
_____
_____

36. How is this situation at the pool of Bethesda unlike those situations where Christ healed multitudes? Pg. 151-152

_____
_____
_____
_____

37. The author writes that it is unfortunate that some do what? Pg. 152

_____
_____
_____
_____
_____

38. Fill in the blanks: Christ's ability to heal the sick was _____ by _____ in a _____ and a _____ sense. Pg. 152

_____

39. The author reminds the reader of situations that illustrate Christ's capacity and limitations were governed by faith. What are they? Pg. 152

_____
_____
_____
_____

40. The next specific event of healing a disability or injury concerns the faith of friends for a disabled man. It is found in Luke 5:17-26. When and where does this miracle take place in Christ's ministry? Pg. 152

_____
_____
_____
_____

41. What does the statement that the author says is unusual seem to imply? What does the author think of this possible implication? Pg. 153

_____

_____

_____

_____

42. What does the author think that Luke wanted to emphasize about Christ? Pg. 153

_____

_____

_____

_____

43. The author draws a comparison with modern healing meetings where an unusually strong presence of the Holy Spirit comes as faith arises in a congregation. Does he believe that this kind of presence is always necessary to heal the sick? Pg. 153

_____

_____

_____

_____

44. Fill in the blanks: Since there were many _____ present, perhaps Luke is telling his readers that the Holy Spirit came with _____ _____ _____ to reveal _____ as _____ on this occasion. Pg. 153

_____

45. Why couldn't the men carrying the man on the stretcher get into the house? Pg. 154

_____

_____

_____

_____

46. Whose faith is noteworthy in this case? How was their faith revealed? Pg. 154

_____

_____

_____

_____

47. Fill in the blanks: While Christ noticed the _____ of the men on the housetop, the _____ of their _____ was the _____ man lying in front of Christ. Pg. 155

_____

48. Fill in the blanks: The _____ of _____ and _____ can release _____ to others perhaps that are not _____ for themselves. Pg. 155

49. Fill in the blanks: Since God alone _____ _____, Christ is taking upon Himself a _____ that God alone _____. This would be _____ if _____ were not God. Pg. 155

50. True or False? Since Christ is God the Son, Christ was speaking the truth about Himself by taking the role of forgiving sins. Pg. 155

51. What was the problem with Christ's religious critics? How is this similar to today? Why does this happen? Pg. 155

52. Christ makes an important connection between forgiveness of sins and healing in this passage. What was it? Pg. 155-156

53. Even though Christ knew that His critics would react negatively, Christ was not bound by what? Pg. 156

54. How did Christ demonstrate that He had authority on earth to forgive sins? Pg. 156

55. What is one way to evaluate the truth of a teaching or a doctrine? Pg. 156

56. Fill in the blanks: The Holy Spirit _____ to the fact that _____ _____ was being _____ by doing _____ _____. Pg. 156

57. Christ described Himself as "Son of Man" in this passage. What is this title generally accepted as? What does Christ's use of this title place emphasis on? Pg. 156

_____

_____

_____

_____

58. What does Christ saying that He had "authority on earth" to forgive sins suggest? Pg. 156

_____

_____

_____

_____

59. Fill in the blanks: Believers have _____ to offer _____ of sins. This does not mean that believers can offer _____ without _____ of _____ or _____. Pg. 156

_____

60. Even Christ did not have _____ to _____ _____ without the _____ _____. Pg. 157

_____

61. Believers stand in _____ _____ releasing people by _____ of the _____ _____ into all of Christ's provision for them in matters of _____ and _____. They become active _____ of _____, confirming, encouraging, and boldly releasing people into the _____ of God provided at the _____ of Christ. Pg. 157

_____

62. According to the author, what is there a "great need" for in our day? Pg. 157

_____

_____

_____

_____

63. What do many people await? Pg. 157

_____

_____

64. What do failures and sins produce? Pg. 157

_____

_____

65. What do those who seek to heal the sick and equip others to heal also find themselves continually dealing with in people? Pg. 157

_____

_____

66. How does the language of the passage indicate that perhaps in this situation of healing that there was an unusual presence of God? What phrases in particular indicate this? Pg. 157

_____

_____

_____

_____

67. The next story that the author covers is the man with dropsy found in Luke 14:1-6. What is dropsy? Pg. 158

_____

_____

_____

_____

68. What day of the week and where did this healing happen? What was Christ doing there? Pg. 158

_____

_____

_____

_____

69. Those in this household were watching Christ closely to find fault with Him. Was Christ afraid to heal this man under these conditions? Pg. 158

_____

_____

70. The author suggests that this situation might have been set up as what? Pg. 159

_____

_____

_____

71. What direct question does Christ ask His critics in this situation? Pg. 159

_____

_____

72. What does the author say is the hidden accusation in this situation? Pg. 159

_____

_____

_____

_____

73. What accusation today is similar? Pg. 159

74. How did Christ answer the question? Pg. 159

_____

_____

75. Fill in the blanks: Christ said that _____ is like the care that one would exercise if their _____ had _____ into a _____ or the _____ that would be exercised to help a _____ _____ fallen into a _____. Pg. 159

_____

76. How is Christ presenting sickness? Pg. 159.

_____

_____

77. How is Christ presenting healing? Pg. 159

_____

_____

78. Why doesn't healing someone on the Sabbath violate the intent of the Law of Moses? Pg. 159-160

_____

_____

_____

_____

79. The next specific event involving healing is the man with a withered hand. It is found in Luke 6:5-11. What day does this healing take place on? Pg. 160

_____

_____

80. What does Christ's bold statement "The Son of Man is Lord of the Sabbath." mean? Pg. 161

_____

_____

_____

_____

81. How does Luke illustrate what Christ means by the bold statement? Pg. 161

_____

_____

82. Does Christ hesitate to heal this man because of fear of criticism? Pg. 161

_____

_____

83. Christ asks His critics a question that presents and compares two choices. What are these two choices? Pg. 161

_____

_____

_____

_____

84. What two phrases does Christ use to describe what that healing the man would be? Pg. 161

_____

_____

85. What two phrases does Christ use to describe what failing to heal the man would be? Pg. 161

_____

_____

86. What answer to Christ's critics is "obvious" according to the author? Pg. 161

_____

_____

87. Fill in the blanks: Christ _____ did _____ in _____ people, despite the amount of _____. Pg. 162

_____

88. What does the author say about people thinking that they can have a healing and miracle ministry without having opposition? Pg. 162.

_____

_____

_____

_____

89. Fill in the blanks: If Christ was _____ in His _____ _____ of the _____ _____, then those who are less than _____ will also _____ _____. Pg. 162

_____

90. The author says that Christ occasionally did what? What should His followers do as a result of this example? Pg. 162

_____

_____

91. Where will some religious opposition often be found? What should anyone wishing to continue to help the suffering do? Pg. 162

_____

_____

_____

_____

92. The last event of healing in this chapter is the High Priest's slave found in Luke 22:50-51. The injury to the slave is mentioned in how many Gospels? How many Gospels mention the healing? Pg. 162

_____

_____

_____

_____

93. The author says that this is the final event of healing before what events? Pg. 163

_____

_____

94. In the face of a threatening mob that had set out to take Christ by force what did Christ demonstrate? Pg. 163

_____

_____

Chapter Ten
Christ Raises the Dead

1. The raising of Jairus' daughter is the first event covered in this chapter. It is found in Luke 8:41-42. How many people did Christ raise from the dead during His earthly ministry? Pg. 164

_____

_____

2. Why does the author say that it is necessary to review this kind of supernatural ministry? Pg. 164

_____

_____

3. What other healing takes place as Christ traveled to Jairus' home? Pg. 164

_____

_____

4. Fill in the blanks: _____ between the beginning and the end of the story of the raising of Jairus' daughter is the _____ of the _____ with the _____ of _____. Pg. 164

_____

5. How did Jairus react after the news that his daughter had died? Pg. 165

_____

_____

6. What did Christ reveal would be the key for his daughter to be made well? Pg. 166

_____

_____

7. What two implications does the author reveal that would apply to any parent facing a serious condition with their child? Pg. 166

_____

_____

8. What two things appear to be opposites in Scripture? Pg. 166

_____

_____

9. How does complex theology cause problems in people's faith? What does it make difficult? Pg. 166

_____

_____

_____
_____
_____
_____

10. Why have some ministers adopted unbelieving theologies when facing a potentially fatal condition in a child? What may they be protecting themselves from? Pg. 166

_____
_____
_____
_____

11. The author lists a number of things that faith is not. What are they? Pg. 166-167

_____
_____
_____
_____

12. Fill in the blanks: Faith simply believes in the _____ of God. Faith is the _____ _____ _____ on the _____ of the Father to _____, _____, and _____ in a specific matter. Pg. 167

_____
_____

13. What does "true faith" obtain? What does "true faith" fight through? Pg. 167

_____
_____
_____
_____

14. What does the author think was the reason that Christ limited the number of people present in the room? Pg. 167

_____
_____

15. According to the author, who laughed when Christ said that the daughter was just sleeping? Pg. 167

_____
_____

16. How did Christ carefully control the conditions for this miracle? Pg. 168

_____
_____

_____

_____

17. What are some alternative translations for the word "spirit" in this passage? Pg. 168

_____

_____

18. The passage says in the New American Standard Version that the daughter's "spirit returned". The author says that what substitution would make sense here? Why? Pg. 168

_____

_____

_____

_____

19. What also would be "a good assumption" according to the author? Pg. 168

_____

_____

_____

_____

20. How long does it appear that this girl been dead? Pg. 168

_____

_____

21. True or False? There seems to be no evidence of specific guidance by the Holy Spirit in the matter of Jairus' daughter. Pg. 168

_____

22. The next resurrection account in Christ's ministry is the resurrection of Lazarus. It is found in Chapter 11, The Gospel of John. The passage begins by telling us of what particular family in what particular village? Pg. 169

_____

_____

23. What evidence is there in this passage that indicates that Christ had a close friendship with this family? Pg. 169

_____

_____

_____

_____

24. Fill in the blanks: Christ's reaction in this situation is _____ _____. Normally, Christ _____ _____ to information like this and _____ the person involved. Christ did not seem to need _____ _____ to respond in that fashion. In contrast,

Christ appeared to have some _____ _____ about this situation that He was _____. Pg. 169

_____

_____

25. The author speculates on how much Christ knew in advance of what exactly was going to happen in this situation. What does he say is "most likely"? Pg. 170

_____

_____

_____

_____

26. What does the author say that there is evidence of in the passage? What does he say that a "careful reading" does not support? Pg. 170

_____

_____

_____

_____

_____

27. Did Lazarus' sickness and death glorify God? Why or why not? Pg. 170

_____

_____

_____

_____

_____

28. What does the author think was the reason that Christ delayed His arrival at Bethany for two days? Pg. 170

_____

_____

_____

_____

_____

29. What figurative language does Christ use to speak of death in this passage? Pg. 171

_____

_____

30. Where else does Christ use this same way of speaking of death? Pg. 171

_____

_____

_____

31. True or False? In resurrections, Christ does nothing more than the actions someone would take in awakening someone from sleep. Pg. 171

_____

32. What should have strengthened the faith of the disciples? Pg. 171

_____

_____

33. When Christ arrives in Bethany, what particular fact reveals that Christ only knew in part? Pg. 172

_____

_____

_____

34. What was Martha's immediate reaction to Christ's presence? Pg. 172

_____

_____

35. Why would Martha have been aware of two events of resurrection in Christ's ministry? Pg. 172

_____

_____

_____

36. How did Christ answer Martha's question as to whether Christ would raise up Lazarus eternally or temporarily? Pg. 173

_____

_____

_____

37. How many times so far in this passage has Christ spoken about believing? Pg. 173

_____

_____

38. How is Mary's initial reaction to Christ's presence similar to Martha's reaction? Pg. 174

_____

_____

39. True or False? Christ often reacted with strong emotions to the hurting people around Him. Pg. 174

_____

40. Some of those who were present used some good logic about Christ. What was it? Pg. 174

41. True or False? The blind are harder to heal than some other conditions. Pg. 175

_____

42. When Christ came to the tomb, there are some indications that Christ might have been receiving divine guidance. What are they? Pg. 176

_____

_____

43. When Christ commands the stone to be removed from Lazarus' tomb how does Martha react? Pg. 176

_____

_____

_____

44. How does Christ respond to Martha's concern above? Pg. 176

_____

_____

_____

45. What condition for this miracle does the question that Christ asked Martha reveal? Pg. 176-177

_____

_____

46. What did Christ pray openly so that the people could hear Him? Pg. 177

_____

_____

_____

47. What has this book repeatedly emphasized a particular truth and purpose since the first chapter? Was the raising of Lazarus was also for the same purpose? Pg. 177

_____

_____

_____

48. Christ loudly commanded Lazarus to come forth. This is like someone trying to do what? Pg. 177

_____

_____

49. What two kinds of reactions did this miracle produce? Pg. 178

_____

_____

50. The last specific incident reviewed in this chapter is the resurrection of the widow's son. It is found in Luke 7:12-17. When does this miracle occur in Christ's ministry? Pg. 178

_____

_____

51. The author says that this event lacks what in comparison with the previous resurrection? Pg. 178

_____

_____

52. True or False? The author thinks that Christ planned this event or knew of it in advance. Pg. 178

_____

53. How did Christ react emotionally to this widow's situation? Pg. 179

_____

_____

54. Fill in the blanks: Christ's _____ for this woman _____ _____ _____ for Him to raise her son from the dead. Pg. 179

_____

55. What action of Christ demonstrates that He believed that He could raise the son from the dead? Pg. 179

_____

_____

56. When should a resurrection occur? What is the longest that someone was buried before resurrection? Pg. 180

_____

_____

_____

_____

Chapter Eleven
Two Incidents of Great Faith

1. The first specific incident is the story of the healing of the Roman centurion's servant. It is found in Matthew Chapter 8. What did Christ say about this centurion's faith? Pg. 181

_____

_____

2. What was the condition of the centurion's servant? Pg. 181

_____

_____

3. What does Christ's immediate reaction to the statement of the Centurion about his servant reveal about the will of God? Pg. 182

_____

_____

_____

_____

_____

4. What did Christ suggest to the Centurion that was the usual pattern of His ministry? Pg. 182

_____

_____

5. What alternative action did the centurion suggest instead? Pg. 182

_____

_____

_____

_____

_____

6. How did the centurion know that it was possible for Christ to command the healing? What did he recognize about Christ's relationship with the Father? Pg. 182

_____

_____

_____

_____

_____

7. How did Christ in two ways endorse the centurion's way of thinking about this healing? Pg. 183

_____

_____

_____

_____

_____

_____

8. Who was in control of this healing? Pg. 183-184

_____

_____

9. Fill in the blanks: The centurion _____ the _____ by his _____ . He received an _____ _____ at a _____ by virtue of his _____ . Pg. 184

_____

_____

10. How did Christ express the truth that the centurion was in control of his miracle? Pg. 184

_____

_____

11. Fill in the blanks: The centurion believed for a _____ _____ and _____ it. Christ did not _____ the _____ that He could _____ at a _____ . Christ was able to do that for which the _____ _____ allowed. Pg. 184

_____

_____

12. How do some react to the truth of the believer's control in matters of healing? Why? Pg. 184

_____

_____

_____

_____

_____

13. How is this shortsighted? What should they encourage those needing healing to do? Pg. 184

_____

_____

_____

_____

14. What happens to the sick and injured when ministers misplace the responsibility back upon the Father? Pg. 184

_____

_____

15. Fill in the blanks: Instead of _____ and _____ their own _____ and _____ in this matter, thereby growing in _____, these ministers may embrace an _____ and _____ doctrine that puts _____ on a supposedly _____ God who is revealing His will in _____ _____ and _____.
Pg. 184

_____

_____

16. By doing the above, they are not seeking to learn from what? Pg. 184

_____

_____

_____

_____

17. The other incident of great faith is found in Mark 5:24-34. It is the story of the woman who had a hemorrhage and bled for twelve years. What had happen financially to this woman in the process of trying to get well? Pg. 184-185

_____

_____

18. What else had her attempts to use natural means to get well done to her? Pg. 185

_____

_____

_____

_____

19. True or False? This woman did not believe that her suffering was a blessing from God. Pg.185

_____

20. What does the phrase "for she thought" indicate about who initiated this situation? Pg. 186.

_____

_____

_____

_____

21. Was there any teaching or encouragement to touch Christ's garments as a means of getting healed? Pg. 186

_____

_____

22. Was there anything special about Christ's clothing? What does this reveal about the nature of God? Pg. 186

_____

_____

_____

_____

_____

_____

23. Fill in the blanks: The Father is not a _____ or an _____ _____. The Father allows believers to _____ the _____ to the _____ or to the presence of _____, and will faithfully reveal Himself in _____ the _____ and _____. Pg. 186

_____

_____

24. How did the woman know that she had been healed? Pg. 186

_____

_____

25. What are some of the most common feelings that accompany healing and miracles? Pg. 186

_____

_____

26. Are these manifestations/feelings necessary to heal the sick? Pg. 186

_____

_____

27. What does God grant manifestations? Pg. 186

_____

_____

28. Fill in the blanks: For the one being healed, faith in Christ as Healer comes _____, then possibly _____, but never _____ first, then _____. Pg. 186

_____

_____

29. Christ also felt something happen in this situation? Pg. 187

_____

_____

30. What other English word comes from the Greek word "dunamis" translated "power" in this event? What would be a literal translation of this word? Pg. 187

_____

_____

_____

31. The author says that "personal experience" allows him to speculate that Christ felt what? Pg. 187

_____

_____

_____

_____

32. Christ knew that someone had been healed but was not clear of what? Pg. 187

_____

_____

33. How do we know that Christ was not in control of this healing? When did Christ know someone was healed? Pg. 187

_____

_____

_____

_____

34. Fill in the blanks: The description of the healing of this woman indicates that when someone is _____ _____ that they will know it either by a _____ of healing or simply by the fact of not having _____ or _____ any longer. Pg. 188

_____

_____

35. What caused this woman's healing according to the words of Christ? Pg. 188

_____

_____

36. Why do some react to the truth about faith? What does the author say about this reaction and the nature of faith? Pg. 188

_____

_____

_____

_____

_____

_____

37. Fill in the blanks: While _____ was the focus of the woman's _____, _____ own will was uninvolved. Christ was _____ of the woman until she was healed. Pg. 188-189

_____

38. Fill in the blanks: Christ does not credit the woman's healing to a _____ _____ who _____ heals people. In fact, the Father had _____ _____ His will: The Father wants people well. Pg. 189

_____

39. Fill in the blanks: The Holy Spirit administered the _____ _____ _____ in response to the _____ _____ in Christ as Healer. Christ credited the _____ _____ in the healing. This was obviously correct as she _____ the whole set of events. Pg. 189

_____

_____

40. What does the author says that it is "apparent" that something was not the cause of the woman's healing? What was it? What then caused her to be healed? Pg. 189

_____

_____

41. Why does the author think that the story of this woman's healing was told repeatedly? Pg. 189

_____

_____

42. True or False? God does not require that faith be expressed only in one fashion in the matter of healing. Pg. 190

_____

43. Why should this story inspire believers? Pg. 190

_____

_____

44. What does the author say that God is not waiting for? Pg. 190

_____

_____

45. Faith for healing is relatively easy if Christians would believe what? Pg. 190

_____

_____

_____

_____

Chapter Twelve
Christ's Followers Heal Specific People

1. The first specific miracle where an individual is identified as being healed by a follower of Christ is found in Acts 3:1-9. Which disciples of Christ are involved in this miracle? Where was this miracle done? Pg. 191-192

_____

_____

2. Who was healed in this situation? Pg. 192

_____

_____

3. The author says that a particular phrase may indicate that Peter received revelation about this particular man. What is that phrase? Pg. 192

_____

_____

4. When Peter did the action above, what did the man think? Pg. 192

_____

_____

5. What did Peter obviously believe he had to give? Pg. 193

_____

_____

6. The author says that Peter's statement is similar to what command of Christ? Pg. 193

_____

_____

_____

_____

7. Fill in the blanks: Believers today also have _____ to _____ in Christ's name and can _____ give _____ away. Pg. 193

_____

8. What did Peter understand about how healing was being done? Pg. 193

_____

_____

9. How did Peter come to understand the Father's will in matters of healing? Pg. 193

_____

_____

10. What do many believers not understand about their authority to do mighty works? Pg. 193-194

_____

_____

11. The man was healed unexpectedly. The author says that this may be another situation of what? Pg. 194

_____

_____

12. Who had overcoming faith in this situation? Pg. 194

_____

_____

13. What does the length of time someone is ill reveal or not reveal about God's will? Pg. 194

_____

_____

14. What sometimes creates a false impression that healing or miracles in the New Testament are done in some other way than faith in Christ? Pg. 194

_____

_____

15. While faith is not mentioned in this account, how do we know faith was involved? Pg. 194

_____

_____

16. The second specific account is Peter's healing of Aeneas at Lydda found in Acts 9:32-35. When does this account happen in relationship with the apostle Paul? Pg. 194-195

_____

_____

17. How long was Aeneas bedridden? Pg. 195

_____

_____

18. Who did Peter say was doing the healing in this case? Pg. 196

_____

_____

19. Peter knew that any healing coming through him was what? Pg. 196

_____

_____

20. Who was manifesting the Father's works? Pg. 196

21. The next specific incident occurs through Peter again. This incident is the resurrection of Tabitha from the dead found in Acts 9:36-42. Where does this resurrection take place? Pg. 196

_____

_____

22. How does the account describe the woman who was involved? Pg. 197

_____

_____

_____

_____

23. Why would the Christians living in Joppa call for Peter? How does this reveal their faith? Pg. 197

_____

_____

_____

_____

24. After Peter's arrives and enters the room where Tabitha's body was laying, how did his actions resemble the Savior's ministry? Pg. 198

_____

_____

25. How did Christ describe death in previous accounts where a resurrection resulted? Pg. 198

_____

_____

26. In those situations, how did Christ produce the resurrections? Pg. 198

_____

_____

27. How did Peter accomplish this resurrection? Pg. 198

_____

_____

28. The next specific event of healing is Paul healing the lame man at Lystra. This account is found in Acts 14:7-15. What were Paul and Barnabus doing when the encountered the lame man who was healed? Pg. 198-199

_____

_____

29. How did Paul know that this man had faith to be made well? Pg. 199-200

_____
_____
_____
_____

30. How did Paul heal the man? Pg. 200

_____
_____
_____
_____
_____

31. How did the people seeing this miracle react to Paul and Barnabus? How did Paul and Barnabus receive this reaction? Pg. 200

_____
_____
_____

32. What did Paul tell them about himself and Barnabus? Pg. 200

_____
_____

33. Why is every believer a candidate to be used by the Father to heal the suffering? Pg. 200

_____
_____

34. The next specific event is Paul's resurrection of Eutychus. It is found in Acts 20:7-12. How was the boy in this story killed? Pg. 200-201

_____
_____

35. How did Paul react to this crisis? How did he resurrect the boy? Pg. 201

_____
_____
_____
_____

36. What always seems to accompany a resurrection? Pg. 202

_____
_____

37. Fill in the blanks: It appears that resurrections may be_____ _____ than healings, but not any _____ _____ from the perspective of the one _____ the _____. Pg. 202

_____

38. Fill in the blanks: Believers must _____ this possibility without acting in _____ _____ and trying to _____ their _____ _____ on other people who are not _____ to believe. Pg. 202

39. Who should be responsible in the matter of a deceased loved one? Pg. 202

40. What "rule of thumb" does the author offer in the matter of praying for a resurrection? Pg. 202

41. The next specific event of healing is Paul's snake-bite miracle. It is found in Acts 28:1-6. What did the natives that observed Paul being bitten think about Paul? Pg. 202-203

42. What is there no evidence of in this passage? Pg. 203

43. What did Paul know about the will of the Father? How did it affect his reaction to this circumstance Pg. 203

44. The final healing in the Acts of the Apostles is Paul healing the father of Publius. This specific event is found in Acts 28:7-9. What was wrong with this man? Pg. 204

45. Who was Publius? Pg. 204

46. Who does the account say healed this man? Pg. 204

47. Why would some react to this if it were not in the Bible? How is this a misguided desire for humility? Pg. 204

_____

_____

_____

_____

48. For most people what is a larger barrier than pride? Pg. 204

_____

_____

49. What are many believers afraid of today? What has caused these fears? Pg. 204-205

_____

_____

_____

50. What is valued more than boldness in many churches today? Pg. 205

_____

_____

51. Fill in the blanks: _____ in matters of healing and miracles is often seen as _____ and _____ is seen as _____ and _____. Pg. 205

_____

52. True or False? Christ has nothing to say about presumption, and has given a great deal of encouragement for bold faith. Pg. 205

_____

53. What should every believer pray for? Pg. 205

_____

_____

54. What should every leader especially do? Pg. 205

_____

_____

_____

55. True or False? The Father will not honor bold mistakes. Pg. 205

_____

56. What do the needs of the last days harvest demand? Pg. 205

_____

_____

_____

_____

Chapter Thirteen
Preaching the Gospel with Signs Following

1. What two different but related activities must a servant of Christ accomplish if he or she wants a Christ-like ministry? Pg. 207

_____

_____

2. Fill in the blanks: Preaching the Gospel with _____ _____ of _____ and _____ must take _____ and is _____ to good teaching. Pg. 207

_____

3. What does anointed teaching do? What is teaching a "backbone" and "preventative" to? Pg. 207

_____

_____

4. What does the New Testament make a "first" distinction between preaching and teaching? Pg. 208

_____

_____

5. What is often connected to preaching the Gospel that is not connected to teaching? Pg. 210

_____

_____

6. What did Paul purposely avoid in preaching the Gospel of Christ? Why? Pg. 211

_____

_____

7. What does Paul intimately connect in 1 Corinthians 1:17-18 with the Gospel? Pg. 211

_____

_____

8. True or False? The cross is not always mentioned in true biblical preaching. Pg. 211

_____

9. What does the preaching of the cross release? What does the Holy Spirit produce in those who believe the Gospel? Pg. 211

_____

_____

_____

_____

10. What was Paul not looking to for help in convincing people of the truth about Jesus Christ? Pg. 212

_____

_____

11. What happens to some preachers? How does this affect their preaching? Pg. 212

_____

_____

_____

_____

12. What was the result of Paul keeping the Gospel simple and focused on the Savior? Pg. 212

_____

_____

_____

_____

13. What two "resting places" does faith have? Pg. 212-213

_____

_____

14. How can a ministry "test" where faith is resting? Pg. 213

_____

_____

_____

_____

15. If scriptural supernatural signs accompany a ministry regularly such as deliverance from evil spirits and healing, then that ministry's faith is likely resting upon what? Pg. 213

_____

_____

_____

_____

16. According to Romans 1:16, what is the dynamic which produces salvation in all its forms? Pg. 213

_____

_____

17. Considering the chart on page 214 in the book. What is the responsibilities on the human side of the equation? Pg. 214

_____

_____

_____

_____

18. Preachers and believers have no responsibility to produce what? Pg. 214

_____

_____

19. True or False? True faith, real believing in the Gospel on the human side of the equation, will result in God releasing power and producing salvation. Pg. 214

_____

20. What must preachers do in order to preach in faith? Pg. 214

_____

_____

21. What has replaced preaching the Gospel in many modern churches? Pg. 215

_____

_____

22. What does proper preaching of the Gospel of Christ do? Pg. 215

_____

_____

23. What does teaching do and not do? Pg. 215

_____

_____

_____

_____

24. What does human wisdom do? Pg. 215

_____

_____

_____

_____

25. Why must teaching take a secondary role? Pg. 215

_____

_____

_____

_____

_____

26. Fill in the blanks: The _____ for teaching will be _____ without the foundation of _____ _____ _____ . Pg. 215

_____

27. What has prevented some who desired deliverance, healing and miracles from accomplishing this? What are they waiting for? Pg. 215

_____

_____

_____

_____

28. True or False? Many leaders no longer see the wisdom in the simplicity of the Gospel. Pg. 215

_____

29. The author says that many ministers overestimate what? Pg. 215

_____

_____

_____

_____

30. Why do these churches seldom see new people in their meetings? Pg. 215-216

_____

_____

_____

_____

31. Why does the average Baptist church grow by evangelism but the average charismatic church grows by transfer growth? Pg. 216

_____

_____

_____

_____

32. Why will the Church rediscover the power of the Gospel? Pg. 216

_____

_____

33. When will the Church be triumphant? Pg. 216

_____

_____

_____

_____

34. What is the Church's scriptural destiny according to the author? Pg. 216

_____

_____

Chapter Fourteen
Healing is an Aspect of Salvation

1. The Greek words that are translated "salvation" and "saved" in most English versions of the New Testament are forms of what Greek word? Pg. 217

_____

_____

2. How many times are forms of this word used in the New Testament? Pg. 217

_____

_____

3. Fill in the blanks: Most English translators will use _____ _____ _____ to express the _____ _____ of _____ in various passages. Pg. 217

_____

_____

4. What aspects of this word do many churches under-emphasize? Pg. 217

_____

_____

5. Fill in the blanks: Deliverance is Christ _____ the believer from _____ _____. Healing is Christ _____ the believer from _____ and _____. Pg. 217

_____

6. What do those exposed to the under-emphasis in these churches often fail to see? Pg. 217

_____

_____

_____

7. What is the basic truth about this word? What else does it mean? Pg. 218

_____

_____

_____

8. How many places are there in the Greek New Testament where a form of the Greek word "sozo" is used in direct reference to some sort of healing? Pg. 218

_____

_____

9. True or False? It is not significant that so many forms of "sozo" have been used in reference to healing. Pg. 218

_____

_____

10. The first place where a form of "sozo" is found in the story of the centurion's slave. The actual Greek word is "diasozo". What does this word mean exactly? Pg. 218-219

_____

_____

11. What is the second place where "diasozo" is used? Pg. 219

_____

_____

_____

_____

12. A parallel passage for Matthew 14:36 where people are being healed by touching Christ's clothing also uses a form of "sozo". Where is this passage found? Pg. 219

_____

_____

13. The story of the woman with an issue of blood occurs in how many Gospels? Pg. 220

_____

_____

14. True or False: The popularity of the story of the woman with the issue of blood may be the reason that so many became inspired to touch Christ's clothing for healing. Pg. 220

_____

_____

15. How many forms of "sozo" are found in the three passages that describe this woman? Pg. 220

_____

_____

16. In all three accounts Christ gives credit to what for the woman's healing? Pg. 220

_____

_____

17. The story of the resurrection of Jairus' daughter appears in how many Gospels and uses forms of "sozo" ? Pg. 221

_____

_____

18. Mark's Gospel relates that Jairus asked Christ for salvation for his dying daughter. What did Christ say that Jairus must do to receive that salvation in the form of healing for His daughter? Pg. 221

_____

_____

19. How many Gospels describe the healing of the blind man Bartimaeus and use forms of "sozo"? Pg. 221

_____

_____

20. What does Christ credit for the healing of Bartimaeus' blind eyes? Pg. 222

_____

_____

21. The story of Christ delivering the demonized man with Legion also uses a form of "sozo". In this case salvation for this insane man included what? Pg. 222

_____

_____

22. How many potential demons were afflicting this man? Pg. 222

_____

_____

23. A form of "sozo" is used in Luke's description of the healing of the ten lepers. What does Christ give credit to in this healing from an infectious disease? Pg. 223

_____

_____

24. After Peter healed the lame man at the Temple, he used a form of "sozo" to explain the healing. How does Peter explain the healing much like Christ does? Pg. 223

_____

_____

25. Paul healed a lame man in Lystra. There is a form of "sozo" found in this account also. What does Paul discern about the man that allows him to minister salvation in the form of healing to him? Pg. 223

_____

_____

26. James also reveals a form of "sozo" in a general encouragement to pray for the sick. He writes that prayer offered in what way will restore the sick? Pg. 224

_____

_____

27. Why have some wanted to disconnect healing from salvation by disconnecting healing from the cross? Pg. 224

_____

_____

28. What should study of the quotation in Isaiah, Chapter 53 that is found in Matthew 8:16-17 do? Pg. 225

_____

_____

29. Who other than Matthew writes that healing was purchased by Christ at the cross? Where is this written? Pg. 225

_____

_____

30. What three witnesses have spoken on the matter that the cross purchases salvation in the form of healing? Pg. 225

_____

_____

31. True or False? The same truths that apply to the forgiveness of sins and regeneration also apply to healing and deliverance? Pg. 225

_____

_____

32. Fill in the blanks: If forgiveness of sins and regeneration are _____ _____ as the Father's will, then healing and deliverance are _____ _____ as well. If the Father _____ wants people saved from sin, then He _____ wants people delivered from demons. If the Father _____ wants to forgive the sins of the _____, then He _____ wants to heal those who _____ His _____ for _____. Pg. 225

_____

_____

33. True or False? The Father's will is settled and never changes in matters of salvation in all its forms including healing. Pg. 225

_____

34. True or False? The only issue is meeting the Father's conditions to receive the Lord Jesus Christ as Savior, Healer, or Deliverer. Pg. 226

_____

35. If faith in Christ as Savior is a condition for receiving forgiveness of sins, then what is required for receiving healing? Pg. 226

_____

_____

36. The author says that the vast majority of people can be healed by what? Pg. 226

_____

_____

_____

_____

37. Fill in the blanks: When these _____ _____ about the will of the Father are _____, then simple but overcoming _____ will be present. Pg. 226

_____

_____

38. True or False? A very few, who seem to have legitimate faith, need to resolve other issues that are blocking the grace of God to them. Pg. 226

_____

39. True or False? The difficulty of a few in receiving healing does not change the fact of the Father wanting them well. Pg. 226

_____

40. What is healing dependent upon? Pg. 226

_____

_____

_____

_____

41. When does healing become predictable and reliable? Pg. 226-227

_____

_____

_____

_____

_____

_____

42. What are some who have misunderstood waiting for in healing? Pg. 227

_____

_____

43. Why is this counterproductive and may block healing? Pg. 227

_____

_____

44. What is the proper timing of forgiveness of sins? Pg. 227

_____

_____

45. Fill in the blanks: The Divine side of the equation is _____. Only the human side of the equation _____ to be _____. Pg. 227

_____

46. True or False? The issue is never the Father's timing but the person's decision to believe in Christ as their personal Savior. Pg. 227

_____

_____

47. When is healing available? Pg. 227

_____

_____

48. What are those seeking healing not trying to do? Pg. 228

_____

_____

49. What has the Father already done for them? Pg. 228

_____

_____

50. What must they do to experience healing? Pg. 228

_____

_____

_____

_____

Chapter Fifteen
Questions and Answers

1. What are the four categories of people healed in Christ ministry? Please answer with a single sentence. Pg. 229-231

A._____

B_____

C_____

D_____

2. Which categories seem to cover the vast majority of those healed in Christ's ministry? Pg. 230

_____

3. Which category seems to be the most unusual and the least frequent way that Christ healed? Pg. 230-231

_____

4. Please summarize. Why can't someone who has the gift of healing empty out a hospital? Pg. 231

_____

_____

_____

_____

5. Please summarize in a single sentences. What are the two categories of people who were not healed in Christ's ministry? Pg. 231-232

A_____

B_____

6. According to the author, what creates condemnation about faith? Pg. 232-233

_____

_____

7. What can happen to a person who was weak in faith yesterday? Pg. 233

_____

_____

8. What could the destruction of a theological doubt accomplish today? Pg. 233

_____

_____

9. What are the four hidden assumptions and problems with of the question: "What about people who have strong faith in Christ as their Healer and have not been healed?"? Pg. 233-235

A._____

B _____

C _____

D _____

10. What is the "blame game"? Pg. 235

_____

_____

11. What four things are largely ignored by complex theology in its consideration of the experience of Job? Pg. 235-239

A _____

B _____

C _____

D _____

12. According to the author, what is one of the Book of Job's best lessons? Pg. 239

_____

_____

13. Why is the blame game harmful to others? Pg. 239

_____

_____

14. What three questions does the author consider in his analysis of the verse that speaks of Paul's thorn in the flesh? Pg. 239

A _____
B _____
C _____

15. The author says that an important truth emerges in this analysis that should help most people's faith. What is it? Pg. 240

_____

_____

16. What was the weakness that Paul was describing according to the author? Pg. 240-241

_____

_____

17. What does the context reveal according to the author? Pg. 241

_____

_____

_____

18. What does the actual verse say that the thorn is? Pg. 241

_____

_____

19. Fill in the blanks: A close analysis of the verse does not reveal that Paul had a _____ or _____. The verse itself reveals that an _____ of _____ was the problem and the context reveals that _____ from _____ is the weakness that Paul asks the Lord to remove. Pg. 243

20. Some have pointed out what they believe to be "four examples of people not being healed in the New Testament". What are these so called "examples"? 243

A_____

B_____

C_____

D_____

21. In the first "example", what two things does the verse *not indicate* according to the author? Pg. 244

A_____

B_____

22. In the first "example", what does the verse indicate according to the author? Pg. 244

_____

23. Fill in the Blank: We can pray in faith for the healing of their wounds and can wisely recommend a _____ _____, a new pair of shoes. Pg. 244

_____

24. In the second "example", did the individual recover from the sickness? Pg. 245

_____

25. In the second example, what word does the author say is often connected with the healing of individuals in the Gospels? Pg. 245

_____

26. The author says that this "example" is not really of someone who was not healed but could be an example of what? Pg. 245

_____

27. Fill in the Blank: The first two examples do beg the question: Does healing from God always have to seem _____ and _____? Pg. 245

_____

28. How does the author answer the question above? Pg. 245

_____

29. The third "example" is about Trophimus. What is the weakness of this verse according to the author? Pg. 245

_____

30. Fill in the Blank: This is a _____ of a moment in time. Pg. 245

_____

31. The author lists four things that we don't know about this situation. What are they? Pg. 245
A_____
B_____
C_____
D_____

32. What one fact can we glean from this situation that the author says is not a surprise? Pg. 245

_____

33. The fourth "example" is similar to the third "example"? What two things do we not know? Pg. 246

_____

_____

34. Fill in the Blanks: This situation is also a snapshot of a _____ _____ in time with no _____ as to what happened afterward. Pg. 246

_____

35. True or False: The fact of Paul being ill, even for a season, does not reveal that the will of God was not to heal him. Pg. 246

_____

36. The author states that these four examples are often cited to support the view that God is selective about who He heals. The author believes that this is a wrong conclusion. What is the right conclusion according to the author? Pg. 246

_____

_____

37. Fill in the Blank: The Church's _____ _____ with healing, good or bad, does not reveal the will of the Father. Pg. 246

_____

38. True/False: Since some in Christ's day did not receive Him as Savior, we must assume that it is God's will not to save all. Pg. 246

39. According to the author, Paul would have never used these verses in the manner that they are being used. Instead of teaching doctrine about healing, what was Paul doing? Pg. 247

_____

40. How was Paul's experience of healing similar to ours? Pg. 247

_____

41. Assuming that it is not the will of God because someone is not immediately healed makes it impossible to do what? Pg. 247

_____

42. Fill in the blanks: Some do not receive _____ _____ or may not receive _____ _____. God is _____ _____ that they receive healing even if they don't receive. Pg. 247

_____

43. Which two of the four "examples" did the believers recover? Pg. 247

_____

44. Which two of the four "examples" do we not know if they received healing eventually? Pg. 247

_____

45. True/False: The assumption that these two were not healed is not based on the New Testament and may reveal a theological bias. Pg. 248

_____

46. Which two of the apostles connect healing with the atonement? Pg. 248

_____

47. What passage in the Old Testament do both of these apostles quote from? Pg. 248

48. Fill in the Blanks: This passage unreservedly mixes verses about _____ with _____ for sin verses. Pg. 248

49. What do some want to balance against this strong double apostolic and prophetic witness? Pg. 248

50. True/False: Silence seems to be a good argument against healing in the atonement. Pg. 248

51. What can we be sure of if healing is *in* the atonement? Pg. 248

52. Fill in the Blanks: If healing is only through the atonement, then healing is only an _____ given at God's _____ _____. Pg. 248

53. Fill in the Blanks: If healing is only through the atonement, then consistent, _____ _____ for healing would be difficult to obtain. Pg. 248

54. The author writes that faith would be based on less than a stable foundation for the one who believes that healing is though the atonement. What would be required then to inspire faith for healing? Pg. 248

55. If healing is *in* the atonement, what can a believer always be sure of ? Pg. 249

56. Isaiah Chapter 53 is connected to what passage in Matthew's Gospel?

57. What two things did Matthew obviously believe according to the author? Pg. 249
A

B

58. Isaiah Chapter 53 is connected to what passage in the writings of the apostle Peter? Pg. 249

59. True/False: First of all, Peter connects the work of the cross very closely to healing in the actual words of the verse above. Pg. 249

_____

60. Fill in the Blanks: Secondly, he (Peter) quotes from the prophecy of Isaiah about _____ that also connects healing with the _____ work of Christ.

_____

61. The author states that the language of Isaiah Chapter 53 does not lend itself to what idea? Pg. 250

_____

_____

62. What phrase in Isaiah Chapter 53 separates the two phrases that Matthew and Peter use in their New Testament quotations? Pg. 250

_____

_____

63. What is this verse unmistakably about? Pg. 250

_____

64. Fill in the Blanks: Isaiah is not _____ healing from the atonement for sin but is _____ them. Pg. 250

65. What is every other statement in these verses about? Pg. 250

_____

_____

66. True/False: To then say that healing is not in the atonement, is an arbitrary statement that is not based on the linguistic facts of this passage (Isaiah Chapter 53). Pg. 250

_____

67. What other fact does the author state is striking evidence that healing is part and parcel of salvation? Pg. 251

_____

68. What often plays a part in the decision to believe that healing is not in the atonement? Pg. 251

_____

69. Fill in the Blanks: Neither _____ nor _____ of sin can be _____ or _____ in people. They must be _____ by an outside observer. Pg. 251

_____

70. True/False: Believing for physical healing cannot be observed or proven. Pg. 252

_____

71. What does the author write that we cannot know or righteously make a judgment about? Pg. 252

_____

72. When someone who appears to believe and has not received healing is interviewed what is often discovered? Pg. 252

_____

_____

73. What alone proves that someone has believed properly in Christ as Healer? Pg. 252

_____

74. True/False: If the Church taught about forgiveness in similar ways that it teaches about healing, then many would have trouble receiving forgiveness. Pg. 252

_____

75. What is not uncommon to see in those who have serious theological doubts about healing in the atonement? Pg. 252

_____

_____

76. Why do some leaders who theoretically believe in healing not want to believe that healing is in the atonement? Pg. 252

_____

_____

_____

_____

77. What are the limitations of the power of suggestion? Pg. 253

_____

_____

_____

_____

78. What kinds of healings could not possibly involve the power of suggestion? Pg. 253-4

_____

_____

_____

_____

79. How does Satan deceive the unwary through healing in false religions? Pg. 254

_____
_____
_____
_____

80. Are manifestations such as falling down or holy laughter always desirable in healing ministry? Pg. 254-255

_____
_____
_____
_____

81. What suggests that we can obtain gifts from God that we don't presently have? Pg. 255

_____
_____
_____
_____
_____
_____
_____

82. What proportion of Christ's healing ministry involved casting out evil spirits causing the sickness or condition? Pg. 255

_____
_____

83. What could be producing the idea that inner emotional healing must occur before physical healing can occur? Pg. 256

_____
_____

84. What kind of "medical care" should be rejected? Pg. 256

_____
_____
_____
_____

85. Why is it easier for people who take good care of their bodies to receive healing? Pg. 257

_____
_____

86. What will cleanse the conscience of one who has abused their body? Pg. 257

87. What have some failed to see about healing? Pg. 257

_____

_____

88. What have some taught that creates faith-destroying doubt? Pg,. 257

_____

_____

89. True/False: Christ never hesitated to heal anyone because they had a health destroying habit. Pg. 257

_____

90. What did Christ compare sickness to? Pg. 258

_____

_____

91. Fill in the Blanks: Christ revealed that the Father is willing to heal _____ who _____ to Him no matter how their condition came and no matter how powerless they are to change their behavior. Pg. 258

_____

92. What is "sudden death syndrome"? Pg. 258

_____

93. True or False? Death can come without sickness or disability being involved. Pg. 258

_____

94. Does the death of a believer by sickness prove that God wished them to die in that manner? Pg. 259

_____

_____

95. Is the death of a believer by sickness a tragedy in an eternal sense? Pg. 259

_____

_____

96. Why does the author think that faith is the primary issue in healing rather than curses, unforgiveness and other things? Pg. 259

_____

_____

_____

97. The author says that there are a few people that may have a hidden desire to remain sick. Why? Pg. 260

_____

_____

98. True/False: The will of God in healing is always done. Pg. 261

_____

99. True/False: The will of God is automatically received without persistence in prayer. Pg. 261

_____

100. What idea is sometimes asserted that the author says is a misuse of the theological idea of God's sovereignty? Pg. 262

_____

101. Fill in the Blanks: Christ revealed the Father's _____ _____ in healing. Pg. 262

_____

102. What idea does the author write that we must not accept? Pg. 262

_____

_____

103. What belief does the author state creates an accusation against God and makes God unfaithful, arbitrary, unpredictable and trustworthy? Pg. 262

_____

_____

104. True/False: The example of Jesus Christ must reveal the Father's ongoing intentions for us all. Pg. 262

_____

105. What does Christ invite us to compare with the Father's desires for us? Pg. 263

_____

_____

106. What does the author believe about our "common sense"? Pg. 263

_____

_____

107. True/False: If we would not injure or make our children ill, then Father will not injure or make us ill either. Pg. 263

_____